HOW TO WEBSITE DESIGN 2026

NO CODING REQUIRED

Glenn Madden

HOW TO WEBSITE DESIGN

Copyright © 2024 Glenn Website Design.

Independently published.

Dedication

I dedicate this book to my family and three children.

I may not have been there for Jessica and David as they grew up but I am very proud they are my children. Tiara was the third and I refused to let her go. I am proud of her also and I am sure she will eventually leave our nest and make a great life.

HOW TO WEBSITE DESIGN

Table of Contents

Introduction

Your No-Code Guide to Building a Killer Website

I know you see it every day — advertisements that promise **"Free Websites," "Build Your Own Site in Minutes,"** or **"Let AI Create Your Website Instantly."**

It all sounds so easy. Well, it is… and it isn't.

When I started building websites back in the **1990s**, things were very different. There were no page builders, no drag-and-drop design tools, and no AI. If you wanted a website, you had to **write every line of code yourself.** I learned **HTML, CSS, JavaScript, PHP**, and a handful of other languages just to get a simple page to appear online. Hosting was expensive, internet speeds were slow, and "responsive design" meant your site might *sort of* work on another computer.

Today, things have gotten much easier — but also much more complex in other ways. The tools are faster, smarter, and often automated, but that doesn't mean you'll automatically end up with a **professional, effective, and profitable** website. Many people fall into the trap of thinking that an instant AI-built website is all they need. In reality, most of those sites are generic, poorly optimized, and disconnected from the unique goals of a real business.

That's where this book comes in.

This book will take you step by step through the **entire process** of building a professional website — not just one that looks nice, but one that actually works for your business. From **choosing a business name, registering a domain, and setting up hosting**, to **designing, writing, optimizing, and promoting** your site, you'll learn how to create a powerful online presence that attracts visitors and turns them into customers.

We'll explore every stage of the journey:

- How to plan your website around your goals and audience.
- How to design with purpose and clarity.
- How to write content that sells.
- How to use tools like WordPress, plugins, analytics, SEO, and AI responsibly.
- How to maintain and grow your site long after it launches.

Whether you're starting your first small business, freelancing, or just want to take control of your online identity, this book will give you the confidence and knowledge to do it right — without wasting time or money on shortcuts that don't last.

The web has changed dramatically since the early days, but one thing remains true:

Success online comes from understanding what you're building and why.

This book is your roadmap to doing exactly that — from your first idea to a fully functioning, future-ready website.

🖥 How To Website Design: From Business Idea to Online Success

A complete step-by-step guide for building, launching, and growing your business online.

Preface

I revised this book in **2024**, back when I was still using AI — ChatGPT specifically — only for light editing and proofreading. A lot has changed since then. Over the past year, I've found myself selling copies of that earlier revision, and every time I did, I felt a little uneasy. Not because it was wrong, but because it was *outdated.*

To tell you the truth, I'm revising this book again **not for profit, not for sales,** but out of a sense of **responsibility.**
In just one year, my entire approach to web design has evolved — almost a full **360-degree turn.** The web changes fast, and so do the tools, methods, and philosophies that drive it. I've learned new techniques, discovered better systems, and adopted ways of thinking that I wish I had included the first time around.

Recently, I made a major shift: I moved all of my websites from a hosting company that was still running outdated server software. That move taught me more than I expected — about performance, reliability, DNS configuration, and how much modern web design now depends on understanding both the *creative* and *technical* sides of hosting.

At the same time, AI has become a serious partner in my workflow. I no longer use it just to check grammar or polish a paragraph. I use it as an **extension of thought**, a brainstorming collaborator, and sometimes even as a design assistant. It doesn't replace experience, but it enhances it.

This new edition reflects all of that — the lessons learned, the mistakes corrected, and the new opportunities that have emerged with AI, automation, and smarter web technologies. If you read the earlier version, you'll notice the difference immediately. If this is your first time picking it up, you'll be getting a modern, field-tested guide to building and maintaining a professional website the right way — from foundation to finish.

I've been designing and managing websites since the **1990s**, and if there's one thing I've learned, it's this:

Every new technology changes how we build — but the principles of good design never change.

This book is my way of sharing those principles with the tools and insights of today.

— *Glenn Keith Madden*

This isn't a sales pitch — it's the truth.
And you may discover that the truth is worth much more than those "Free Website" or "AI builds it in minutes" offers.

If you do, contact me. Advice is **free** — but yes, I also build websites customized for each client's needs.

That *was* a sales pitch.

Glenn Website Design

https://glennwebsitedesign.com

PART I – FOUNDATION: FROM VISION TO NAME

Chapter 1 – Why Every Business Needs a Website

Explains why a modern website is essential for credibility, visibility, and customer trust. Covers the psychology of first impressions online, how websites outperform social media pages, and why every serious business must control its own digital "home base."

The Basics Never Change

The basics will never change. But how you achieve those goals does — on a daily basis.

Over the years, I've watched website design shift from hand-coded HTML to AI-assisted page builders, from dial-up connections to global cloud networks. Yet the same timeless principles still define every successful website.

Whether you're building your first site or your fiftieth, remember that the foundation of success always includes:

1. **Clarity** – Visitors must instantly understand who you are and what you offer.
2. **Credibility** – Your design, writing, and details should inspire trust at a glance.
3. **Usability** – Make navigation effortless; people should never have to think about how to find something.
4. **Relevance** – Keep your content fresh, accurate, and valuable to your audience.
5. **Speed and Access** – Fast loading and mobile-friendly design are no longer optional.
6. **Consistency** – Maintain a unified look, tone, and message across all pages.
7. **Engagement** – Always give visitors a reason to stay longer or come back — a story, a product, or a benefit that connects with them.

How you deliver those basics has changed — we now use tools, automation, and AI that make it faster and easier — but **what makes a great website has not.**

The technology may evolve daily, but the principles of honesty, clarity, and service remain the true constants of web design.

Unless you have a product that is so unique, so in demand that everyone in the world already wants it, you need a website.

Living in Indonesia, I can't count how many times I've searched for a business on Google Maps, clicked the "Website" link, and ended up on an **Instagram account** instead. That's common practice here. But for me — an American who's been working online since the late 1990s — it's a red flag.

If a business doesn't have even the simplest website, I instantly lose confidence. To me, it signals either a lack of professionalism, a lack of stability, or simply a lack of understanding about how the modern marketplace works. A **website is your handshake in the digital world.** It tells potential customers, "We're real. We're here. You can trust us."

Even a free or basic site looks more credible than an Instagram page or Facebook profile. Those platforms are useful tools, but they are **rented space.** You don't own them — and the moment the algorithm changes or your account gets restricted, your digital storefront disappears. A website, on the other hand, is property you control. It's your online headquarters, your 24-hour salesperson, and your most powerful marketing asset.

Digital Storefront vs. Physical Presence

I've been running an online presence since **1998** and have **never had a physical storefront** of my own. Yet I've sold products, shipped containers of furniture worldwide, and maintained a network of customers across multiple continents. The secret? My websites were open for business even when I was asleep.

You don't need a showroom to prove you're real — but you do need a **physical address and professional contact details** to establish legitimacy. I manage this by partnering with a trusted friend in the United States who serves as my official U.S. address for correspondence and trust verification.

The beauty of the internet is that your website *is* your store. You can invite the world in without needing to sweep the floor or unlock the door. The key difference is that while a physical storefront depends on passing foot traffic, a **digital storefront depends on search traffic** — and that means your website must exist, be optimized, and communicate your credibility instantly.

How Customers Search and Make Decisions

Think about how *you* look for services today. When you need a new supplier, a restaurant, or even a dentist, where do you go? You search online.

Your potential customers are doing the same thing. They're comparing prices, reviews, and — most importantly — **the quality of your website.**
A well-designed site gives instant reassurance that your business is organized, active, and professional. A missing or outdated site, on the other hand, plants doubt in their mind:

"Are they still in business?"
"Why can't I find more info?"
"Maybe I'll check the next one…"

People rarely say these words out loud, but subconsciously, they make the decision in seconds.

Modern consumers judge credibility within the **first 5–7 seconds** of landing on a page. Your design, layout, and tone tell them whether to stay or leave. Even small businesses with limited budgets can compete if they present themselves clearly and confidently.

Trust, Visibility, and Credibility Online

Trust online is built through three layers:

1. **Visibility** – Can people find you?
2. **Credibility** – Do you look professional and reliable?
3. **Consistency** – Do you deliver what your website promises?

A business with no website fails at all three. Even if you rely on social media, those platforms limit your visibility to followers or algorithmic luck. A website allows you to appear in **search results**, build long-term SEO, and serve as the foundation for your Google Business listing, customer reviews, and marketing campaigns.

Having your own website also protects your reputation. Anyone can create a fake social profile in your business's name — but your **domain name and SSL certificate** prove authenticity. That's something customers subconsciously notice when they see the little lock icon in their browser.

Trust online is cumulative: a clean design, clear contact details, testimonials, and consistent branding all work together to make visitors feel secure.

Case Studies: Small Sites That Outperformed Big Brands

Over the years, I've seen small websites consistently outperform major brands simply because they understood their audience.

A furniture maker with a single-page website showcasing high-quality photos and straightforward pricing can attract more genuine buyers than a large manufacturer with a confusing, outdated catalog site. Why? Because clarity converts.

Similarly, a small tutoring company that publishes helpful blog posts answering real student questions can outrank international education platforms on Google — simply by providing valuable, focused content.

The web is an equalizer. It doesn't matter how big your company is — **it matters how well you communicate.**

The Website as Your 24-Hour Salesperson

Your website doesn't sleep, take weekends off, or call in sick. It works **24 hours a day, 7 days a week, 365 days a year.**

Every page is an opportunity to make an impression, answer a question, or close a sale. A properly designed website:

- Welcomes visitors with professionalism
- Explains what you offer clearly
- Answers common objections before they're asked
- Guides visitors to take the next step

It's like having a perfectly trained salesperson who never gets tired and never forgets what to say. And unlike traditional advertising, it doesn't keep costing you every time someone clicks — it continues to build value over time.

When done right, your website becomes your **most loyal employee** — one that introduces your business to the world, builds trust, and drives revenue while you focus on growth.

Key Takeaway

In today's digital economy, having no website is like having no sign on your store.
Social media alone is not enough.
A website isn't just about being online — it's about **being found, trusted, and remembered.**

Chapter 2 – Defining Your Purpose and Audience

Guides readers through clarifying their goals—whether to sell products, promote services, or build a personal brand—and identifying the ideal audience. Includes simple exercises for matching business intent with site design and messaging.

Before you begin building anything — before you choose a theme, buy hosting, or write your first sentence of text — you need to answer one critical question:

"What is the purpose of this website?"

Most people skip this step. They start by focusing on colors, logos, and layouts, and end up with a site that *looks* good but doesn't *do* anything.
A professional website must be built with purpose, not guesswork. Every design choice, every menu item, and every paragraph of text should serve a clear goal.

This chapter helps you define that goal — and identify exactly who you're trying to reach.

Clarifying What Your Website Should Achieve

A website can have dozens of features, but at its core, it should do one or two things **exceptionally well**.
Ask yourself honestly:

- Do I want to **sell** something?
- Do I want to **get inquiries or leads**?
- Do I want to **educate and build trust**?
- Do I want to **showcase my work or story**?

Each purpose changes the design approach completely.
For example:

- A **product-based business** needs clear images, pricing, and purchase options.
- A **service-based business** needs testimonials, booking links, and proof of expertise.
- A **personal brand or creator** needs storytelling, professional photos, and strong social integration.

It's okay for your website to grow into multiple purposes later, but at the beginning, focus on **one core outcome** — something measurable like:

- "I want people to fill out my contact form."
- "I want to sell five products a week."
- "I want visitors to subscribe to my newsletter."

Everything else — layout, color, content, and even plugins — should be chosen to support that goal.

Identifying Your Ideal Visitor

Once you know what you want your website to do, you need to understand **who** it's for.

Too many small business websites try to speak to everyone — and end up connecting with no one. The best websites feel personal because they're written as if they're speaking directly to a single type of person.

Start by describing your ideal visitor as if they were sitting across from you:

- Who are they? (age, gender, location, profession)
- What are they trying to accomplish?
- What problems or frustrations are they dealing with?
- How do they usually search for what you offer?
- What words or tone would make them feel understood?

Here's an example from my own experience:
When I design a website for **furniture buyers**, my ideal customer isn't just "someone who likes furniture." It's a professional, usually in their 40s–60s, who appreciates craftsmanship, has a home project or business interior to complete, and prefers long-lasting quality over mass-produced trends.
Knowing this helps me write the right kind of content — focused on craftsmanship, trust, and shipping reliability — instead of just posting photos of chairs.

You can't communicate effectively until you understand **who you're talking to.**

Mapping Goals to Website Types

Now that you have your goal and your audience, you can choose the right *type* of website. Each serves a distinct purpose and influences both your design and content strategy.

Website Type	Main Purpose	Best For
E-commerce Site	Sell products directly online	Retailers, artisans, or manufacturers
Portfolio Site	Showcase work, skills, or services	Designers, photographers, writers, freelancers
Lead-Generation Site	Collect contact info or inquiries	Consultants, agencies, real estate, coaching
Blog or Content Site	Build authority, SEO traffic, and trust	Educators, writers, affiliate marketers
Corporate / Brand Site	Present company identity and information	Established businesses, manufacturers, service providers
Landing Page / Funnel	Drive a single focused action	Campaigns, product launches, signups

A website without a clear type is like a shop without shelves — people walk in, look around, and leave confused.
Choosing the right category helps you prioritize what matters most. For instance:

- A **portfolio** site should make the work easy to browse.
- An **e-commerce** site must simplify the buying process.
- A **lead-generation** site should make contacting you effortless.

If you're unsure, start small with your main objective and expand later.

It's always easier to add complexity than to fix confusion.

Common Early Mistakes and How to Avoid Them

When starting out, most business owners fall into one (or more) of these traps:

1. Trying to Please Everyone

You can't serve every audience. If you try, you'll dilute your message.
Speak directly to your ideal customer. Everyone else will respect you for having focus.

2. Building Without a Strategy

Jumping straight into design tools without planning your purpose or structure leads to wasted time.
Sketch your goals first. Your website should be built like a house — blueprints before bricks.

3. Copying Competitors Blindly

It's fine to study other websites for inspiration, but don't duplicate their structure or tone without knowing if it fits your market.
You don't know what's *working* for them — or what's not.

4. Ignoring the User's Journey

The average visitor lands on your site looking for a quick answer. If you make them hunt for it, they'll leave.
Map out a clear visitor flow: *Where do they start? What do they click next? What do you want them to do at the end?*

5. Forgetting the "Why"

Over time, websites tend to drift away from their original mission. Revisit your purpose regularly.
If your goals or audience change, your website must evolve too.

Simple Exercise: The One Sentence Test

Write one sentence that defines your website's purpose, audience, and goal.
For example:

"This website helps homeowners find and order custom mahogany furniture directly from our workshop in Indonesia, showcasing our craftsmanship and making the buying process simple and trustworthy."

If you can't summarize it clearly in one sentence, you're not ready to design yet.

Once you can, you've just written the foundation of your homepage headline.

Key Takeaway

Before you build, design, or write anything, define **what success looks like** for your website — and who it's for.
A well-defined purpose gives your website direction.
A clearly understood audience gives it a voice.
Together, they turn a simple page into a powerful business tool.

Chapter 3 – Choosing the Right Business Name

Shows how to brainstorm memorable, SEO-friendly names that resonate with your audience. Discusses naming conventions, domain availability, and ensuring cross-platform consistency across social media and branding materials.

Your business name is more than just a label — it's the first impression you make, the anchor for your website, and the foundation of your brand identity. It's how people will remember you, search for you, and talk about you.

Choosing the right name is both art and strategy. A strong name not only fits your vision but also works technically — across your domain, social media, and marketing materials.

This chapter will show you how to brainstorm a memorable, SEO-friendly, and brandable business name that sets you apart and keeps your online presence consistent everywhere.

Naming Strategies (Descriptive, Invented, Hybrid — but NOT Keyword-Stuffed)

When people start thinking about naming their website, they often rush to include keywords like *furniture*, *design*, or *photography* in the domain. It might seem like a good SEO shortcut, but that thinking is outdated — and potentially harmful.

My advice: **stay away from keyword-heavy domain names.**

Over the years, I've owned and operated dozens of websites across different industries, and I've consistently seen that keyword-based domains often get **less traffic** than my short, branded ones. Why? Because Google and users both value trust and identity more than generic matches.

A Personal Example: NESOE.com

When I launched my teaching platform, I didn't call it *OnlineEnglishTeacher.com* or *EnglishLessonsForJapan.com*. Instead, I created **NESOE.com**, which stands for **Native English Speaker Online Education**.

It met all the right criteria:

- **Short** – just five letters. Easy to type and remember.
- **Memorable** – unique enough to stand out in any conversation.
- **No trademark conflicts** – simple to verify and safe to use globally.
- **Brandable** – something I can grow and expand without being trapped by keywords.
- **Relevant** – the meaning connects naturally with what I do.

That single choice gave me flexibility. I can expand NESOE into courses, audio programs, and teacher collaborations — all under one brand. If I had used *EnglishOnlineLessons.com*, I'd be stuck with a name that sounds like every other site in the same space.

A strong business name should **create identity, not describe function.**

Understanding the Keyword Myth

In the early days of Google, having a keyword in your domain name gave an immediate ranking boost. For example, *BuyShoesOnline.com* might automatically rank higher for "buy shoes online." But that shortcut disappeared more than a decade ago.

The Google EMD Update (Exact Match Domain)

In **September 2012**, Google released the **Exact Match Domain (EMD) update**, changing the game completely.

Purpose:
To penalize low-quality websites that used keyword-stuffed domain names to trick search results.

Impact:
After this update, many thin or spammy sites with keyword-based domains dropped in rankings overnight. Google shifted its focus toward **content quality, user experience, and relevance.**

Continuing Evolution:
By **2024**, leaked internal documents confirmed that Google still includes a **demotion factor** for exact match domains. That means having a domain that perfectly matches a keyword (like *BestShoesOnline.com*) can actually hurt you if your content doesn't meet high-quality standards.

So, while keywords in a domain aren't automatically bad, they no longer hold the weight they once did — and in some cases, they can do more harm than good.

The Current Situation for Exact Match Domains

Let's be clear: there's nothing inherently wrong with having a keyword in your domain if it fits your brand naturally.

For example, **AloYoga.com** includes "yoga," but it's clearly a brand — not a keyword play. The domain supports a company identity, not just a search term.

Today, **Google ranks brands, not just websites.**
That means:

- A keyword domain alone won't help you.
- A branded domain with great content, strong reputation, and backlinks will.

How to Brainstorm the Right Name

Here's a simple, practical approach to naming:

1. **Start with meaning.**
   Write down words that reflect your values, tone, or industry — but not necessarily what you sell.
   Example: *growth, clarity, motion, craft, trust, origin.*

2. **Blend or invent.**
   Combine fragments of words or create something entirely new.
   Example: *Spotify* (spot + identify), *Verizon* (veritas + horizon), *Nesoe* (acronym-based).

3. **Check pronunciation.**
   If people can't say it easily, they won't remember it.

4. **Keep it short.**
   Under 12 characters is ideal; avoid hyphens and numbers.

5. **Test memorability.**
   Say it aloud. Tell a friend once. Ask them 10 minutes later if they remember it. If they do, you've got something good.

6. **Imagine it on merchandise.**
   Could you print it on a T-shirt, business card, or shipping label and still look professional?

Checking for Trademarks and Conflicts

Before you fall in love with a name, make sure it's **legally safe.**
Here's how:

- Search your country's trademark database (e.g., USPTO.gov for the U.S.).

- Do a Google search for existing companies using similar names.

- Check domain registrars and social media handles.

- Avoid anything too close to an established brand — even if it's spelled differently.

Trademark issues can cost you far more than rebranding early.

Branding Consistency Across Web and Social

Once you've chosen a name, consistency is everything.
Make sure your name is:

- **Available as a domain** (ideally .com, but .co or .io can work).

- **Consistent on social platforms** (Instagram, X, Facebook, LinkedIn, YouTube).

- **Identical in your logo, tagline, and email.**

If possible, register the same username across all platforms, even if you don't plan to use them yet. This prevents confusion and helps your customers find you anywhere.

Your website, social media, and emails should all look and sound like they belong to one brand — not three different businesses sharing the same name.

Tools for Testing Name Availability and Memorability

Here are a few tools I use and recommend:

- **Namecheap / GoDaddy / Porkbun** – to check domain availability.

- **Trademarkia.com** – for trademark search and monitoring.

- **Knowem.com** – to check social media username availability.

- **Google Trends** – to test public interest or associations with similar words.

- **ChatGPT / AI tools** – for creative brainstorming and checking word meanings or translations.

Use these to confirm your name is unique, safe, and ready to brand.

Branding Recognition and Longevity

Building brand recognition takes time. You won't see instant results the day you launch your website, but if your name is strong and your work consistent, recognition builds momentum.

Once your audience associates your name with trust and quality, it becomes a multiplier — every new product, website, or service you release under that brand inherits credibility automatically.

That's why **building a brandable name is an investment, not an expense.** It opens doors that keyword-heavy shortcuts never will.

Key Takeaway

Your business name is the first step toward owning your identity online.

Avoid chasing search shortcuts — build something memorable instead.

A great name is:

- Short, brandable, and easy to remember
- Unique and legally safe
- Consistent across all platforms
- Backed by real value and quality

The domain name may be your address, but your brand name is your reputation.

Choose it carefully — it will carry everything you build from here on.

Chapter 4 – Securing Your Domain Name

Your domain name is your online address — the gateway between your brand and the world. You can have the best products, the sharpest design, and the most optimized content, but if your domain isn't properly registered and protected, you're building on sand.

This chapter will show you how to secure your domain name the right way — choosing the best extension, registering it safely, maintaining privacy, and ensuring it always points exactly where you want it to go.

Domain Extensions (.com, .co, .ai, etc.) and Which Fit Your Business

There are now hundreds of **Top-Level Domains (TLDs)** — everything from .com and .net to .ai, .io, .design, and even .coffee. The right one depends largely on your business type, your target audience, and your branding goals.

Here's a quick guide:

TLD	Typical Use	Notes
.com	Commercial businesses	Still the most trusted and recognized extension worldwide.
.net	Tech, infrastructure, networks	Once popular; now secondary to .com.
.org	Nonprofits, organizations	Best for causes, communities, and NGOs.
.co	Startups, companies	Seen as a modern .com alternative.
.ai	Artificial Intelligence, tech, and innovation	Popular for AI startups; adds a tech-savvy

TLD	Typical Use	Notes
	brands	image.
.io	Software, apps, and developer projects	Common in tech circles; short and trendy.
.shop / .store	E-commerce and retail	Signals a product-focused site immediately.
Country codes (.us, .uk, .id, .de)	Local or regional businesses	Helps with local SEO and trust in specific markets.

For most businesses, **.com is still king.**
It's what people instinctively type and what search engines recognize as the most credible. But if your niche is tech or AI-related, a specialized extension like .ai can fit perfectly and even feel more current.

A good way to decide is to **Google your competitors** and note what extensions they're using. You'll quickly see what's standard in your market — and where you can stand out.

How to Check Availability and Register Properly

The domain registration process is simple, but it's easy to overlook critical details. Follow this step-by-step approach:

1. **Search smart.**
   Use registrars like **Namecheap, Google Domains, Porkbun,** or **Moniker** (my personal choice) to check name availability. Most will also show you alternative extensions automatically.

2. **Register directly, not through middlemen.**
   Avoid buying your domain through web builders like Wix or Squarespace. It's better to **own your domain independently** so you can move hosting freely without complications.

3. **Register for multiple years.**
   Secure at least two to five years upfront. It's cheaper in the long run and prevents losing your name due to an overlooked renewal.

4. **Use a reliable registrar.**
   I personally use **Moniker** as my registrar and recently moved my hosting to **DreamHost**, which has performed far better with modern server technology. The key is reliability — choose companies that have been around for years and have transparent control panels.

5. **Keep ownership in your name.**
   Double-check the WHOIS information after purchase. Make sure your **name and email** are listed as the registrant — not a web designer, agency, or hosting company. You'd be surprised how many businesses lose control of their own domain because they let someone else register it for them.

Privacy Protection and DNS Basics

Every domain has public information attached to it, known as **WHOIS data**, which includes the registrant's name, address, phone, and email. To prevent spam, data theft, or unwanted contact, use **domain privacy protection** (often called "WHOIS Guard" or "Private Registration").

Most registrars offer it free now. Always enable it unless you intentionally want your business info to be public.

Understanding DNS

DNS (Domain Name System) is what connects your domain name to your website's actual location on the internet — its **IP address**.

Here's a simplified breakdown:

- **A Record:** Points your domain to your hosting server.
- **CNAME Record:** Used for subdomains (like blog.yourdomain.com).
- **MX Record:** Directs email to the right server (essential for @yourdomain.com mail).
- **TXT Record:** Used for verification (like Google Search Console or email security).

You don't have to be an expert to manage DNS, but knowing what each record does helps you troubleshoot problems faster and keep your site online smoothly.

Handling Multiple Domains and Redirects

It's common — and often wise — to register multiple domain names that relate to your main brand. You can then use **redirects** so that every visitor ends up at your primary website.

For example, I manage **TiffanyLampsForSale.com** — a long-standing site — and I also own **TiffanyTableLamps.com**, which redirects to the main site. I bought it to capture alternative search traffic and protect my brand name from competitors.

Just to be clear, I purchased **TiffanyLampsForSale.com** *long before* Google downgraded keyword-rich names. Back then, it made perfect sense. But as search engines evolved, I learned that brand power matters more than domain phrasing.

If you use multiple domains, remember:

- **Redirect everything to one canonical address —** usually your main .com site.

- **Avoid duplicate content —** don't host the same site on multiple domains.

- **Use 301 redirects** for permanent forwarding to preserve SEO value.

Buying related domains also helps with **brand protection —** no one else can purchase similar names to impersonate or compete with you.

Avoiding Scams and Bad Domain Deals

Domain reselling is a billion-dollar business, and while there are legitimate aftermarket sites, many sellers inflate prices or use manipulative tactics.

Watch out for:

- **Emails claiming your domain is about to expire** — always verify directly with your registrar.
- **"Urgent" upgrade offers** from unknown registrars.
- **Domains listed for resale at extreme prices** — if it's over $1,000, think carefully before buying. There's almost always an alternative.

Unless a domain has extraordinary strategic value, **never overpay.** Focus your resources on building your content and reputation instead.

Pro Tip: Secure Related Variations

If you can, buy:

- Common misspellings of your domain
- Your domain with both **.com** and your country code (e.g., .us, .id)
- Shortened versions or relevant brand variations

Set them all to redirect to your main website. It's inexpensive insurance against confusion or copycats.

Key Takeaway

Your domain name is your most important digital asset — treat it like property.

Register it yourself, keep it secure, and renew it on time.

Remember:

- .com is still the gold standard, but choose a TLD that fits your brand.
- Always enable privacy protection.
- Learn the basics of DNS to stay in control.
- Use redirects strategically for brand protection.
- Never let anyone else own your digital identity.

A domain is more than a name — it's your flag planted on the internet. Make sure it's flying where *you* want it to.

PART II – HOSTING, TOOLS & SETUP
Chapter 5 – Understanding Web Hosting

When you visit a website, what you're really doing is connecting to a **server** somewhere in the world that stores its files and delivers them to your browser. That server — and the company that maintains it — is your *web host*.

Hosting determines how fast your website loads, how secure it is, and how reliably it stays online. You can have a beautiful design and powerful content, but if your host is slow or outdated, visitors will leave before they ever see it.

My Own Experience: Why I Switched Hosts

One of the biggest reasons I decided to revise this book was my own recent hosting overhaul.

For over **20 years**, I used **iPower** for more than **30 websites.** They served me well for a long time, but after their parent company changed ownership in 2021, priorities shifted from *service* to *profit*. Support slowed, reliability dropped, and — most critically — the servers were never upgraded beyond **PHP 7.4**.

That was the final straw.

PHP 7.4 officially **reached end-of-life on November 28, 2022**, meaning it no longer receives **security patches or bug fixes**. Any site running on it is exposed to known vulnerabilities that hackers actively exploit.

If your hosting company hasn't updated to **PHP 8.1, 8.2, or 8.3**, you are putting your data, your visitors, and your reputation at risk.

I moved everything to **DreamHost**, a provider that stays current, uses modern server software, and offers dedicated support. The difference was immediate — faster load times, better uptime, and stronger overall stability.

That experience reinforced a lesson every site owner needs to remember:

Good hosting is not an expense — it's the foundation of your business.

Types of Hosting Explained

Different businesses have different hosting needs. Here's a breakdown of the four main types of hosting and how to choose the right one.

1. Shared Hosting

- Multiple websites share the same server and its resources.
- Cheapest and easiest to start with.
- Ideal for beginners, blogs, or small business sites.
- Downsides: slower performance, limited control, and higher security risks if another site on the same server is compromised.

2. VPS (Virtual Private Server)

- One physical server is divided into several isolated virtual servers.
- Each account gets dedicated resources and higher stability.
- Best for small to medium businesses with moderate traffic.
- More control and scalability than shared hosting, but also more technical to manage.

3. Dedicated Server

- You rent an entire physical server just for your websites.
- Maximum power, control, and security.
- Perfect for large e-commerce sites or enterprises with high traffic.
- Expensive and often requires professional server management.

4. Cloud Hosting

- Your website runs on a cluster of connected servers rather than one machine.
- Automatically scales resources up or down as traffic changes.
- Great for growing businesses and tech startups.
- High uptime, flexible pricing, but requires some setup knowledge.

If you're just starting, **shared hosting** is fine — but choose a reputable company that offers easy upgrades later. As your site grows, you can move up to VPS or Cloud hosting for better performance.

Bandwidth, Uptime, and Storage

To understand hosting properly, you need to know a few basic terms:

Bandwidth

This is how much data your website can transfer each month. Every image, video, or page view uses some bandwidth. If you exceed your plan, your host may slow your site down or charge extra.

Tip: Choose *unmetered* or *scalable* bandwidth if you expect growth.

Uptime

This measures how often your site is online, expressed as a percentage. A good host guarantees **99.9% uptime** or better (less than nine hours of downtime per year).

Storage

This is the amount of space available for your files, images, databases, and emails. Most small business sites use less than 20 GB. E-commerce or media-heavy sites may need 50 GB or more.

SSL Certificates

These encrypt communication between your website and visitors. Always use SSL. Most hosts now include **Let's Encrypt SSL** for free.

Choosing Hosting for Your Growth Plan

Before buying hosting, ask yourself:

- How much traffic do I expect in the first year?
- Will I need professional email accounts?
- Do I plan to host multiple websites?
- Do I want automatic backups and updates, or can I manage them manually?

Start small, but pick a host that allows you to **upgrade easily**. You should be able to scale from a shared plan to VPS or cloud hosting without rebuilding your website.

My Real-World Setup

I currently host all my sites on **DreamHost**, using a mix of shared and VPS accounts.

- Shared plans handle smaller projects and teaching sites.
- VPS plans run my main e-commerce brands that need extra performance.
- Daily automatic backups and one-click restores protect everything.

That mix gives me both speed and flexibility without overspending.

Top 5 Hosting Providers in 2025

Here are five trusted companies I personally recommend or have tested, each with a specific strength:

1. DreamHost

- Offers shared, VPS, dedicated, and cloud hosting.
- Fast SSD drives, free SSL, and up-to-date PHP versions.
- Transparent pricing with reliable U.S.-based support.
- Best for multi-site owners and WordPress users.

2. SiteGround

- Known for fast servers, excellent customer support, and built-in caching.
- Ideal for WordPress and WooCommerce stores.
- Slightly higher price but unmatched performance and uptime.

3. A2 Hosting

- Focused on speed with "Turbo" servers optimized for PHP 8+.
- Great choice for developers and growing small businesses.
- Offers both affordable shared plans and powerful VPS options.

4. Hostinger

- Affordable entry-level shared and cloud hosting.
- Modern control panel and global data centers.
- Perfect for startups, personal projects, and budget-conscious users.
- Limited phone support, but excellent value overall.

5. WP Engine

- Premium managed WordPress hosting only.
- Handles all technical maintenance automatically.
- Outstanding reliability and speed, but priced for businesses rather than hobbyists.

Each of these companies supports modern PHP versions and strong security standards. The right one depends on your technical comfort level and budget.

Beware of "Unlimited" and Other Hosting Traps

Many hosting companies advertise features that sound impossible to beat:

"Unlimited Websites."
"Unlimited Bandwidth."
"Unlimited Email Accounts."

Here's what they don't tell you.

The Inode Limit

Every host secretly enforces an **inode limit** (sometimes called a *file usage limit*).

An inode is simply a count of everything stored on your account — each file, folder, and email counts as one.
When you hit your limit, you can't upload files or even receive new emails.

Shared hosting plans often cap inodes around **150,000 to 300,000**. If you run multiple WordPress sites, store images, or keep large backups, you'll reach that quickly.

Before signing up, read your host's **resource usage policy** to find the actual inode limit.

The "Unlimited" Bandwidth Illusion

"Unlimited bandwidth" doesn't mean infinite speed. It usually means "unmetered until you use too much."

If your site suddenly spikes in traffic, your host may **throttle** (slow down) your connection or temporarily **suspend** your account.

True unlimited bandwidth only exists in cloud systems that bill per usage.

The Biggest Trap: The Renewal Surprise

Most hosting companies offer low first-year prices — sometimes 70% off — to hook new customers.
What they don't highlight is the **year-two price jump**, which can double or triple your cost overnight.

A $2.99/month plan often renews at **$8.99–$10.99/month**. Add privacy protection and domain renewal, and your yearly bill skyrockets.

Protect yourself:

- Always check the *renewal rate* before purchase.
- Consider locking in a multi-year plan at the intro rate if you're sure about the host.
- Plan your budget for the *second year*, not just the first.
- Keep your site's file count lean and delete unused backups or emails to stay under inode limits.

Avoiding Common Hosting Mistakes

1. **Choosing purely by lowest price** – Cheap hosts overload their servers, causing slow sites.

2. **Letting your web designer own the hosting** – Always keep billing and control in your own name.

3. **Ignoring backups** – Set automatic daily backups or use a WordPress plugin like UpdraftPlus.

4. **Running outdated software** – Keep PHP, WordPress, and plugins updated for security.

5. **Not testing before launching** – Use a staging area or subdomain to safely test updates.

Don't Let Convenience Trap You

Many people lose control of their own websites simply because they took the "easy route."
Signing up through a website builder, reseller, or bundled package might seem convenient, but it often means **you don't truly own your hosting account, your files, or even your domain.**

If the provider closes, merges, or changes its terms, you can lose years of work overnight.
I've seen businesses vanish from the internet because they didn't have direct access to their hosting login or backup files.

Always make sure that:

- The hosting account is **registered in your name** with your own email address.

- You have **independent access** to the control panel and billing.

- You keep **off-server backups** (on a local drive or cloud storage you control).

43

- You understand how to move your site to another host if needed.

Convenience can be expensive. Take the time to learn the basics and keep ownership in your hands — because losing your website is more than losing files; it's losing your customers, your brand, and your credibility.

Final Warning: The Add-On Trap

Before you finish choosing a host, there's one more thing to watch out for — **add-ons**.

Many hosting companies love to pad the checkout process with extra products you don't need. You'll see boxes for things like *Website Builder Packages, Advanced Security Suites, SEO Boosters, Email Pro Plans,* and even "priority support" upgrades. These can easily double your cost without adding real value.

I'll be honest — I personally **hate GoDaddy** for exactly this reason. I'm not saying they're bad today (it's been years since I last tested them), but their checkout pages used to be a maze of upsells. You'd start with a $3.99/month hosting plan and somehow end up at $15/month after clicking "continue."

The truth is, many of these "premium features" are already included with other hosts as standard. For example:

- **Free SSL** — now standard at nearly every reputable provider.
- **Basic website builder tools** — available free in WordPress.
- **Email accounts** — often included or cheaper through Google Workspace or Zoho.
- **Backup tools and malware scans** — free plugins handle this better.

Some hosts also push unnecessary **paid website design or marketing packages** that sound tempting to beginners but deliver little lasting benefit.

So before you check out, look carefully at the order summary. Uncheck everything that isn't essential. You can always add more features later, once you know exactly what you need.

Remember:

A good host doesn't nickel-and-dime you — it gives you everything you need in one honest plan.

Do your homework, avoid the upsell traps, and keep control of both your hosting and your budget from day one.

Key Takeaway

Your host is your invisible partner in every success or failure online.

- Keep your software and PHP versions current.
- Expect 99.9% uptime and free SSL by default.
- Read the fine print on "unlimited" offers.
- Plan for renewal costs and future growth.

Good hosting isn't about who's cheapest — it's about who keeps your website safe, fast, and always open for business.

Chapter 6 – Setting Up Your Environment

Once you've chosen your hosting provider and secured your domain, the next step is setting everything up so your website actually comes to life. This process may sound technical, but once you understand the basics, it becomes routine.

Your goal in this stage is to connect your domain to your hosting, secure it with SSL, install your website platform (usually WordPress), and configure email, backups, and essential tools.

If your hosting company is good, all of this will be easy to set up.

Why You Should Register Your Domain with an Official Registrar

Nearly every hosting company will offer to register your domain for you at checkout. It sounds convenient — one payment, one login, everything in one place. But that convenience can turn into a **trap** if you ever decide to change hosts.

When your host controls your domain registration, they control your ability to move it. Transferring can become slow or complicated, and if something happens to your hosting account, you may even lose access to your domain.

That's why I **always register my domains through an official registrar**, not through my hosting company.

Personally, I use **Moniker**, which has been an **ICANN-accredited registrar** for decades. I switched to them because they specialize in domain management — that's their business — and they've consistently been cheaper than what iPower used to charge.

A dedicated registrar ensures:

- Your domains remain independent of your hosting provider.

- Transfers between hosts are quick and easy.

- You maintain full ownership and control of your names.

- Renewal reminders are clear, and prices are transparent.

Think of your registrar as your **domain bank** and your hosting company as your **digital warehouse**. You can store your assets anywhere, but your title should always stay in your name.

Linking Your Domain to Hosting (DNS, A & AAAA Records, SSL)

If you use a separate registrar like Moniker, connecting your domain to your hosting is simple.

Your hosting company will give you two or more **nameservers**, such as:
ns1.yourhost.com and ns2.yourhost.com

Log into your registrar account, find the DNS settings for your domain, and replace the existing nameservers with the ones provided by your host. It usually takes a few hours for these changes to propagate globally.

Once connected, you can also manually manage **DNS records** if needed:

- **A Record:** Points your domain to your website's IP address.

- **AAAA Record:** Same as A record but for IPv6 addresses.

- **CNAME Record:** Points subdomains (like blog.yourdomain.com) to another domain.

- **MX Record:** Directs email traffic to the right mail server.

After your DNS is set, the next step is to **install SSL**. Most modern hosts (like DreamHost, SiteGround, or A2 Hosting) include **Let's Encrypt SSL certificates for free.**

Activate it immediately — not only does it encrypt your data, but it also prevents Google from flagging your site as "Not Secure."

Installing WordPress or an Equivalent CMS

For most people today, **WordPress** remains the best and most flexible content management system (CMS). It's free, powerful, and supported by a massive global community.

Your host likely offers a **one-click WordPress installer**, which sets everything up in minutes. During installation, choose a strong admin password, and make sure your username is not "admin." Hackers target that default.

Over the years, I've stripped my own websites down to a **bare-bones setup** — the fewer moving parts, the faster and safer the site runs. WordPress plugins are powerful, but too many of them can slow your site down and create conflicts.

Here's my current minimal setup — proven, reliable, and lightweight:

- **Theme: NEVE (with upgrade)** – Fast, responsive, and easy to customize.
- **Jetpack:** Offers performance, security, and stats. I use it sparingly because its security module can sometimes conflict with other tools.
- **All-in-One WP Migration & Backup:** The easiest backup and migration plugin available.
- **All-in-One WP Migration Unlimited Extension:** Allows large backups and full site transfers.
- **Otter – Page Builder Blocks & Extensions for Gutenberg:** Excellent for flexible page design using WordPress's native block editor.

- **WPForms:** A must-have for creating enquiry or contact forms without exposing your email address. This reduces spam dramatically.

- **WP Mail SMTP:** Essential. WordPress's default PHP mail system often fails because many email providers block PHP mail for security reasons. SMTP (Simple Mail Transfer Protocol) ensures reliable delivery through services like Gmail, Sendinblue, or your host's mail server.

- **Yoast SEO:** Critical for optimizing your titles, descriptions, and structure for Google.

That's all you really need to build a fast, secure, professional WordPress site. Everything else is optional.

File Management (FTP, cPanel, and Backups)

Even if you rely on your host's dashboard for most tasks, it's worth understanding basic file management.

cPanel (Control Panel) is a web-based dashboard most hosting companies provide. It lets you manage:

- Files and folders
- Email accounts
- Databases
- DNS settings
- Backup and restore functions

If your host doesn't use cPanel, they'll have their own version (DreamHost, for example, uses a custom panel), but the features are similar.

You can also connect directly to your hosting files using **FTP (File Transfer Protocol)** or **SFTP (Secure FTP)**.
I recommend using a client like **FileZilla**. It gives you direct access to your site's root directory so you can upload files, edit configuration settings, or delete unused backups manually.

Always keep **two types of backups**:

1. **Automatic server backups** (your host should provide daily or weekly options).
2. **Offline backups** (using All-in-One WP Migration or similar, saved to your computer or cloud drive).

Having both ensures you can recover your website no matter what happens — even if your host has a major failure.

How to Avoid Common Beginner Configuration Errors

When setting up your environment, here are a few beginner mistakes that can cost you time and stress:

1. **Installing too many plugins.**
   Every plugin adds load time and risk of conflict. Use only what you need.
2. **Ignoring SSL setup.**
   Without it, browsers will warn visitors that your site is insecure, which destroys trust instantly.
3. **Using "admin" as your username.**
   Hackers target that first. Always use a unique username.
4. **Skipping backups.**
   Don't wait until your site breaks to realize you never made one.
5. **Leaving the default tagline.**
   Many new WordPress installs still say "Just another WordPress site." Change it immediately to your slogan or key phrase.
6. **Forgetting to test your email.**
   Send yourself a test through your site's contact form to make sure SMTP is working correctly.

7. **Not deleting sample pages or plugins.**
   "Hello World" and "Sample Page" make your site look unfinished and unprofessional.

8. **Failing to update themes and plugins.**
   Outdated software is the number one cause of hacked WordPress sites. Always keep everything updated.

Final Thoughts

Setting up your environment might feel like a chore, but it's where the foundation of your website's stability is built. Once your domain, SSL, WordPress, and email are all properly configured, you'll have complete control — not just a website that "works," but one that's secure, optimized, and ready to grow.

You'll find that if your hosting company is good, **everything connects easily**. A few minutes spent doing it right now will save you hours of frustration later.

Chapter 7 – Planning Your Site Architecture

"Fail to plan, plan to fail."

That saying has never been more true than when setting up an online business presence.

The internet is full of half-finished websites — great ideas that never found structure. A website without a clear plan is like a building without blueprints: it might look fine from the front, but sooner or later, it collapses under its own confusion.

Planning your site architecture — how your pages are organized, linked, and experienced — is the most overlooked yet most powerful step in web design.

Do this right, and everything else will fall into place. Do it wrong, and no amount of SEO, plugins, or paid ads will fix it.

Why Site Architecture Matters

A well-structured website helps both humans and search engines understand what your business is about. It guides visitors from curiosity to action, making sure every page has a purpose and every link helps people find what they're looking for.

Good architecture means:

- Visitors can find what they need in **three clicks or less.**
- Google can crawl and index your pages efficiently.
- You can expand easily later without breaking your menu or links.
- Your brand feels organized, professional, and trustworthy.

Before you install a single plugin or upload a photo, take the time to design your **digital blueprint.**

Pages Every Business Needs

While every company is unique, most professional websites share a few essential pages. These form your site's core — the structure from which everything else grows.

1. Home

Your front door. It should summarize your business, capture attention, and guide visitors toward your most important content. Think of it as your **elevator pitch** online — clear, simple, and instantly engaging.

2. About

People want to know who they're dealing with.
Share your story, your values, and what makes your company different. Include photos, team introductions, or even a short founder's note.

3. Services or Products

The heart of your business.
If you offer multiple services, give each its own page. This helps SEO and makes navigation cleaner.

4. Contact

Make it easy to reach you — not just with a form, but also with visible email, phone, and location details (if applicable).
Add Google Maps integration for local businesses.

5. Blog or Resources

This is your opportunity to build authority and improve SEO. Regular posts show search engines and visitors that your site is active and knowledgeable.

6. Privacy Policy & Terms

If you collect emails, run ads, or use cookies, you're legally required to have these. They also show professionalism and transparency.

Depending on your business type, you might also include:

- Portfolio / Gallery
- Testimonials / Reviews
- FAQ
- Pricing
- Shop or Booking System

The goal is to give visitors exactly what they need without overwhelming them.

Hierarchy, Menus, and Internal Linking

Your **site hierarchy** is the structure of how pages relate to each other — your "family tree."

A simple example:

Home
↳ About
↳ Services
    ↳ Web Design
    ↳ SEO
    ↳ Maintenance
↳ Blog
↳ Contact

Your **navigation menu** should reflect this hierarchy. Keep it short — ideally 5 to 7 main links. Too many menu items can confuse visitors and clutter your design.

Tips for Menus and Links

- Keep primary navigation at the top or in a sidebar.

- Include a **footer menu** for secondary pages like Privacy Policy, Terms, or FAQs.

- Use **internal links** naturally within your content — for example, linking "website optimization" in your blog post to your Services page.

- Every page should have a clear "next step," such as a call-to-action button or related links.

Good internal linking not only improves user experience but also boosts SEO by helping Google understand which pages are most important.

Wireframes, Flowcharts, and Sitemap Tools

Before you start building, visualize your layout. This step saves hours later.

A **wireframe** is a simple sketch or digital mockup that shows where each element will go on a page — logo, menu, text, images, buttons, footer.

A **flowchart** maps how visitors will move through your site — from landing page to checkout or contact form.

You don't need expensive software to do this. Free and easy tools can make the process fast and even fun.

Recommended Free Tools

I maintain a list of my favorite free web design and SEO tools here:

☞ https://glennwebsitedesign.com/free-seo-tools/

From sitemap generators to keyword planners and page analyzers, these are the same tools I use when planning or optimizing client websites.

Other helpful tools:

- **Draw.io or Lucidchart** – For flowcharts and navigation planning.
- **Figma or Canva** – For creating simple wireframes.
- **Google Sheets** – For outlining your page structure and tracking content status.
- **Yoast SEO plugin** – For generating XML sitemaps automatically once your site is live.

Even a hand-drawn sketch on paper is better than no plan at all. The point is to **see** your structure before you start building it.

Accessibility and User Experience (UX) Foundations

Accessibility isn't just about meeting regulations — it's about respecting your audience.
A site that's easy to read, navigate, and interact with builds trust and widens your reach.

Key accessibility and UX basics:

- Use **clear fonts** and strong contrast between text and background.
- Ensure your site works well on mobile devices — over half of all web traffic is mobile now.
- Add **alt text** to images for users who rely on screen readers (and for SEO).
- Avoid color-coding information without text labels — colorblind users will miss it.
- Test your navigation with real users. If they can't find something in under ten seconds, fix it.

A good rule of thumb:

If someone who's never seen your site before can find what they want easily, your UX is working.

Simple Exercise: Build Your Site Blueprint

Before you open WordPress or install a single plugin, create a one-page document called **"Website Blueprint."**

Include:

- Your main goals (e.g., sell products, generate leads, build authority)
- A list of all planned pages
- The main menu structure
- Each page's purpose
- Notes on visuals, tone, or special features

This simple document becomes your roadmap. You'll refer to it constantly during the build.

Final Thoughts

Planning isn't exciting, but it's the step that separates amateurs from professionals.

A clear site structure saves you hours of frustration, helps visitors trust your brand, and tells Google exactly what your site is about.

When you plan well, building becomes simple.
When you skip planning, building becomes endless.

PART III – DESIGN & CONTENT CREATION

Chapter 8 – Designing with Purpose

Designing a website isn't about decoration — it's about direction. Every color, font, image, and layout choice should guide visitors toward your purpose. A website that looks nice but confuses people will lose business faster than one that looks simple but communicates clearly.

Good design builds trust. It makes people comfortable. It tells them, "You're in the right place."

And in today's world, **design starts with the user's screen —** not the designer's desk.

Responsive Design: The World in a Smaller Screen

I'll be honest: this part took me, an "old-timer," a while to adapt to.

When cell phones first became internet browsers, I did what many people my age did — I resisted.

I stuck with my old text-based phone for years. I still have it in a drawer somewhere, a fossil from a simpler time. I was actually angry when my older daughter bought my daughter, Tiara, her first iPhone. I saw what was coming: distraction, screen addiction, a world where conversation shifted to swipes and taps.

And yes — much of that came true. But so did something else: **the complete transformation of how people interact with information.**

Today, the younger generation is *born* connected. They use phones for everything — shopping, banking, learning, dating, and yes, even seeking advice before they make a purchase.

If your website isn't built with that in mind, you're invisible to most of your potential audience.

Over 60% of web traffic now comes from mobile devices.
That means if your site doesn't load correctly, doesn't fit the

screen, or takes too long to open on a phone, visitors won't wait. They'll move on instantly.

Building with **responsive design** — a layout that adapts automatically to any screen size — is no longer optional. It's survival.

Layout Fundamentals: Visual Hierarchy, Whitespace, and Balance

When someone lands on your website, their eyes start scanning immediately.

They don't read line by line; they look for meaning and structure.

Your design should guide them gently from what's most important to what's next.

Here are the fundamentals that never change:

1. Visual Hierarchy

Decide what matters most on each page and make it stand out.

- Use **larger headlines** for key ideas.
- Highlight your call-to-action buttons with contrasting colors.
- Keep secondary elements smaller or lighter.

Your visitors should always know where to look first — and where to click next.

2. Whitespace

Whitespace (or negative space) isn't wasted space — it's breathing room.

It separates elements, adds elegance, and makes reading easier.

Crowded pages make visitors anxious; open layouts make them relax.

3. Balance

Balance doesn't mean symmetry — it means harmony.

If one side of a page feels heavy with text or color, balance it with open space or a strong image.

Your goal is a calm rhythm that feels natural as someone scrolls.

Choosing Themes or Frameworks Wisely

In WordPress, your **theme** is your foundation. It controls your site's layout, design style, and sometimes its speed.

Don't just pick a theme because it looks flashy in the preview. Choose one that's:

- **Lightweight** – A theme bloated with scripts will slow you down.
- **Responsive** – It must look great on desktop, tablet, and mobile.
- **Supported** – Check that it's updated regularly and compatible with PHP 8+.
- **Customizable** – You should be able to change colors, fonts, and layouts easily without coding.

Personally, I use the **NEVE theme** (with upgrade). It's fast, stable, and flexible — ideal for both professional and personal websites.

Avoid themes that come loaded with built-in sliders, galleries, and "demo content." They may look great at first but often cause performance problems later.

If you're building multiple sites or planning to scale, consider a **framework** (like GeneratePress or Astra). They allow deep customization without having to rebuild your site from scratch.

Mobile-First and Responsive Design Principles

Modern web design starts with **mobile-first thinking**. Instead of designing a big desktop site and then shrinking it for phones, design for phones first — then expand for larger screens.

Why? Because on mobile:

- Attention spans are shorter.
- Space is limited.
- Speed is everything.

Mobile-First Design Tips

- Keep menus short and clear.
- Use larger buttons for easy tapping.
- Avoid hover-based effects (they don't exist on touchscreens).
- Compress images for faster loading.
- Place your most important message **above the fold** (visible without scrolling).

Once your site works beautifully on a phone, scaling up to tablet and desktop is easy.

And one rule I've learned the hard way:

Build on a desktop, **but test, test, test** on multiple screen sizes and devices.

Use your phone, your tablet, and even a friend's device. What looks perfect on one screen can break completely on another.

If your hosting includes staging or preview modes, use them — they save embarrassment later.

Color Psychology and Brand Tone

Colors speak before words do. They influence emotion, trust, and even purchasing decisions.

Here's a quick guide to what colors generally communicate:

- **Blue:** Trust, calm, professionalism (used by banks and tech companies)
- **Red:** Energy, excitement, urgency (great for sales or bold brands)
- **Green:** Growth, health, and nature (common for wellness and eco brands)
- **Black:** Luxury, authority, sophistication
- **Yellow:** Optimism, creativity, warmth
- **White or Neutral tones:** Simplicity, cleanliness, openness

Choose your color palette based on the **feeling you want your visitors to have** when they land on your site.
If your brand is creative and upbeat, bright colors work. If it's luxury or serious, stick with minimal palettes and bold accents.

Keep consistency across your pages — your logo, buttons, and headings should share the same visual language.
And remember: color contrast isn't just about style — it's about **readability** and **accessibility**.

Simple Exercise: The First Impression Test

After designing your homepage, ask a friend or colleague to open it for five seconds.
Then ask them:

1. What do you think this site is about?
2. What would you click on first?
3. How does it make you feel?

If they can't answer quickly, your design needs refining.
Good design communicates instantly, before a single word is read.

Final Thoughts

The devices may have changed, but design fundamentals haven't.

Balance, color, clarity, and purpose still rule the craft — we just view them through smaller screens now.

You don't have to be a designer to make a beautiful website. You just need to **respect your visitor's time** and make your message clear on any device they use.

I may still miss the simplicity of those old flip phones, but I can't deny the truth:

The world now lives on mobile screens — and success online belongs to those who design for it.

Chapter 9 – Crafting Your Content

Your website design attracts visitors.
Your content keeps them there — and convinces them to act.

This chapter is about turning words into results: writing text that builds trust, explains your offer, and gently guides your visitor to take the next step.

You don't need to be a professional writer to create great website content. You just need clarity, honesty, and a little help from modern tools — including AI.

Writing for Clarity, Persuasion, and SEO

Up until now, AI hasn't played a huge role in this process. But this is where you'll use it most — and where it can truly shine.

AI can help you write clear, professional content, and if you use it regularly, it will even start learning your personal writing style.

You can feed it your older blog posts, social media captions, or product descriptions to help it mimic your voice.

But remember this:

AI can assist you, but it can't *replace* your voice.

Use AI to draft, brainstorm, or reword ideas — but always review the text yourself. Add your personal insight, tone, and experience. That's what separates a genuine business from a generic one.

Good content balances three key goals:

1. **Clarity** – Make your message instantly understandable.
2. **Persuasion** – Encourage action without pressure.
3. **SEO** – Write naturally while including words your customers actually search for.

How to Structure Headlines and Calls-to-Action

Headlines are the most powerful words on your site. Most visitors only skim them, so they must deliver your message fast.

Headlines

- Be specific, not vague.
  Instead of "Welcome to Our Website," write "Custom Mahogany Furniture, Handcrafted for You."
- Use action words: *Discover, Learn, Create, Save, Build.*
- Keep them short — under 70 characters for SEO.

Subheadings

Break up text every few paragraphs. Subheadings make scanning easy and help search engines understand your structure.

Calls-to-Action (CTAs)

Every page should have a clear "next step." Examples:

- **Shop Now**
- **Get a Free Quote**
- **Schedule a Call**
- **Download the Guide**

Make your CTAs visible and consistent. If you're selling products, place buttons near the top of the page and again after your main description. If you're offering services, end each section with a prompt to contact you.

Remember: visitors don't want to "figure out" what to do — they want to be *guided.*

Image Selection and Compression

Visuals often speak louder than text.
High-quality images add credibility, while poor or slow-loading ones do the opposite.

Choosing the right images:

- Use **original photos** whenever possible — they build trust.

- If using stock photos, choose ones that look authentic and match your brand tone. Avoid overly staged or generic shots.

- Keep all images in **landscape orientation** unless vertical shape is required (like product galleries).

- Add **alt text** to every image — this helps SEO and accessibility.

Compressing for speed:

- Before uploading, reduce file sizes using free tools like **TinyPNG** or **Squoosh**.

- Aim for images under 300KB whenever possible.

- Large hero images can be up to 1MB if optimized well.

Remember: a slow site kills conversions.
Every second of extra load time can drop your conversion rate by up to 20%.

Video and Multimedia Integration

Videos can dramatically increase engagement if used thoughtfully. They humanize your brand and let people "meet" you before contacting you.

Keep these principles in mind:

- Keep videos **under two minutes** unless they're tutorials.
- Host them on **YouTube or Vimeo** and embed them — don't upload large files directly to your hosting server.
- Add **captions** or subtitles; many people watch with sound off.
- Include a **short description** or title for context.

Interactive media (like 360° product views or testimonial videos) can boost trust, but don't overuse them. Too many moving elements distract from your message.
Use video to *support* your content, not compete with it.

Blending SEO Naturally

We'll dive deeper into SEO later, but the foundation begins here. In fact, SEO starts all the way back when you picked your **host** — a fast, secure server already gives you an edge.

But now, as you write, SEO becomes your compass for how people find you.

Keyword Research

The best tool I've found for keyword discovery is **Google Keyword Planner**, now part of Google Ads. You'll need to create an account, but using it for research is free.
It shows you:

- What terms people are searching for

- How often they're searched
- How competitive each keyword is

Use it to learn how your **future customers** are finding your **competitors.** That's your roadmap to the words that matter.

Writing with Keywords

- Choose 1–2 main keywords per page.
- Place them in the title, first paragraph, subheadings, and meta description.
- Use variations naturally throughout the text.

Avoid overdoing it.

Keyword stuffing (repeating the same phrase too often) makes writing sound robotic and can actually hurt your ranking. Google now ranks pages for *meaning* and *intent*, not repetition.

If your writing reads smoothly to a human, you're doing SEO correctly.

Writing for Your Buyer — Not for Everyone

The most successful websites sound like they're speaking directly to *you*.
That's because they are.

Know your ideal customer. Write for them, not for the crowd.

For example:

- A furniture buyer wants quality, craftsmanship, and reliability.
- A language student wants confidence, progress, and a friendly tone.
- A tech startup wants innovation and performance.

Each group responds to different words, emotions, and examples.

Use the same tone your customer would use if they were explaining their problem to you.
If they speak casually, write casually. If they're professionals, use precise, confident language.

The golden rule:

Write like you talk — but cleaner.

Simple Exercise: The "Customer Conversation"

Imagine your best potential customer sitting across the table. Write down five questions they would ask about your product or service.
Now, answer them — conversationally, honestly, and clearly.

Congratulations — you've just written the foundation of your website's copy.

Final Thoughts

Your content is your conversation with the world.
AI can help you speak more clearly, but *you* provide the meaning.

Be authentic. Use your customer's language. Blend keywords naturally. And always, always end each page with a clear next step.

When design and content work together, your website stops being just a brochure — it becomes your best salesperson.

Chapter 10 – Photography and Media Essentials

A website's visuals speak before a single word is read. The colors, photos, and videos you choose instantly communicate your quality, tone, and credibility. In the online world, people decide in seconds whether to trust what they see — long before they start reading what you say.

"A picture is worth a thousand words,"
and on the internet, it might also be worth a thousand clicks.

This chapter will help you choose and prepare the right visuals so your site looks professional, loads quickly, and earns trust.

Sourcing Royalty-Free vs. Original Photos

Stock photos are useful — but only when chosen wisely. I use **Pixabay** for most of my free, royalty-free images. It's one of the best libraries for clean, modern photos that don't look overly staged.

Sometimes, though, you need something more specific or higher quality. That's when it's worth paying for **Shutterstock** or another premium site. Just be very careful when setting up your account.

I learned the hard way — once, what looked like a "free trial" quietly turned into a **one-year recurring subscription.** Always read the small print before entering payment information.

Here's a good rule of thumb:

- **Use free sites** (Pixabay, Pexels, Unsplash) for general imagery and backgrounds.
- **Use paid libraries** (Shutterstock, Adobe Stock) for niche, brand-critical visuals.
- **Use your own photos** whenever possible — they build authenticity better than anything else.

People trust what looks real. If you can photograph your actual products, workspace, or team, that's always the best investment.

Optimizing Image Size and Alt Tags

Beautiful photos can destroy a website if they're too large. Slow-loading pages drive users away and hurt your search ranking.

Optimization Tips

1. Resize images before uploading — keep them around **1200 px wide** for standard web use.
2. Compress using tools like **TinyPNG**, **Squoosh**, or **ImageOptim**.
3. Save in modern formats like **WebP** when possible.
4. Use **alt tags** — short text descriptions that tell search engines and screen readers what each image shows.

Alt tags are both an accessibility feature and an SEO booster. Example:

Instead of *"IMG_1043.jpg"*, use *"handcrafted-mahogany-resolute-desk-detail.jpg"* and add an alt tag like *"Close-up of carved mahogany panel on Resolute Desk."*

Integrating Product Galleries or Slideshows

For online stores or visual portfolios, a good gallery makes all the difference.

Tips for effective galleries:

- Show multiple angles or variations of the same product.
- Use a clean lightbox or slider plugin that doesn't autoplay too quickly.
- Keep file sizes small so images load instantly.
- Include short captions or titles — people remember descriptions paired with visuals.

If you're using WordPress, look for lightweight gallery plugins such as **FooGallery**, **Modula**, or even the built-in Gutenberg gallery block. Avoid flashy sliders that add unnecessary scripts; simplicity always performs better.

Intro to AI Image Tools (and Their Limitations)

AI-generated images are improving rapidly, but they're still imperfect.

I've experimented with many — and to be honest, I've had **very little luck**.

There's almost always a flaw: text misspelled, fingers missing, proportions off, or details that just look "off."

AI tools like **DALL-E**, **Midjourney**, and **Stable Diffusion** can be fun for concepts, mockups, or filler images, but not for professional products or people shots.
They're great for brainstorming layout ideas or background textures — not for your homepage hero image.

If you decide to use AI-generated art, always:

- Double-check licensing rights.
- Inspect every pixel before publishing.
- Avoid using AI photos that could misrepresent your real products or customers.

AI visuals can complement your content — but they shouldn't replace genuine photography.

Why Visuals Matter More Than Ever

Your potential customer's attention span is short — **less than 8 seconds** on average. That means your images must instantly communicate what your business does and why it matters.

Ask yourself:

- Does this photo tell the right story?
- Does it load quickly on a phone?
- Does it reflect my brand tone — calm, bold, luxurious, playful?

The right photo grabs attention. The wrong one sends people looking elsewhere.

Simple Exercise: The Two-Second Scan

Open your homepage and glance at it for just two seconds. Without reading any text, ask yourself:

1. What message do I get from the visuals alone?
2. Do I instantly know what this business does?
3. Would I feel confident buying from this brand?

If you can answer "yes" to all three, your images are doing their job.

Final Thoughts

Great visuals don't just decorate a website — they **define** it. They communicate your story, your professionalism, and your personality faster than any paragraph ever could.

Whether you shoot your own photos, use stock images, or experiment with AI, the goal is the same:

Show people what you stand for, before they scroll or read a single word.

Choose wisely, compress carefully, and test everything. A website that looks sharp and loads fast builds the kind of first impression that keeps customers coming back.

Chapter 11 – Building Pages in WordPress

Now that your website environment is ready — domain connected, hosting secure, and WordPress installed — it's time to actually *build*.

This chapter will walk you through creating pages, menus, forms, and navigation using WordPress's modern tools. Whether you're using the Gutenberg block editor or a page builder like Elementor, the goal is the same: to create a clean, fast, easy-to-navigate site that's both functional and secure.

Blocks, Classic Editor, and Page Builders

In WordPress, everything you see on a page — text, images, buttons, or forms — is built from **blocks**.
The Gutenberg editor introduced this system years ago, replacing the old "Classic Editor" that looked more like a word processor.

At first, many long-time designers resisted the block editor (myself included), but once you get used to it, it's faster, lighter, and better for SEO.

You can mix and match different block types:

- Paragraph, image, video, or gallery
- Buttons, forms, and columns
- Lists, quotes, and embeds

Using Page Builders

Some designers prefer **Elementor**, **Divi**, or other visual drag-and-drop builders. Elementor, in particular, has great assets and templates — and it's very beginner-friendly.

However, it can also become **expensive** and **bloated** if you're managing multiple sites or complex layouts.

I personally use the **Otter plugin**, which gives me powerful design blocks inside Gutenberg — essentially doing what Elementor does, but directly within WordPress's native editor. It's lightweight, fast, and doesn't lock you into a proprietary system.

If I need to add a simple image slider, I use **Smart Slider**, a reliable plugin that integrates easily with Gutenberg.

The key takeaway:

Choose the simplest tool that does what you need — and nothing more. Every extra plugin adds complexity and load time.

Creating Menus, Categories, and Sidebars

Your **theme** determines how menus and sidebars appear, but the structure itself is managed inside WordPress.

To set up a menu:

1. Go to **Appearance → Menus**.
2. Create a new menu (for example, "Main Navigation").
3. Add pages, categories, or custom links.
4. Assign it to the correct location (usually "Primary Menu").

Keep it simple. A clean, focused menu improves both user experience and SEO.
Five to seven items is usually perfect.

Categories are primarily for organizing blog posts or products. They help visitors browse related content and help Google understand your site's topics.

Sidebars are optional but useful for displaying:

- Search boxes
- Recent posts
- Promotions or ads
- Contact buttons

Most modern themes let you customize sidebars using **widgets** (found under Appearance → Widgets).

If your theme supports full-site editing (like Neve or Astra), you can create custom headers, footers, and widget areas directly from the visual editor.

Integrating Forms, Contact Pages, and Maps

Every professional website needs an easy way for people to get in touch.

The simplest and most secure solution is to use **WPForms** — one of the best form builders available for WordPress.

It lets you create:

- Contact forms
- Quote request forms
- Newsletter sign-ups
- Feedback forms

You can start with a free version, and if needed, upgrade later for more advanced features like conditional logic or file uploads.

For **email delivery**, pair it with **WP Mail SMTP**. This plugin routes your site's outgoing mail through a secure SMTP service instead of the unreliable default PHP mail function (which many email providers block).

It ensures that messages from your contact form actually reach your inbox instead of disappearing into spam filters.

If your business has a physical location, embed a **Google Map** on your contact page.

This adds both trust and convenience for customers trying to find you.

Securing Pages with Plugins and SSL

Security starts the moment your site goes live. If you followed the earlier steps, your host should already have provided **free SSL** through Let's Encrypt. Make sure your site address begins with https:// — not http://.

Beyond SSL, you'll need some basic protection against spam, malware, and brute-force login attempts.

I use **Jetpack** for this.
It's a multipurpose plugin from WordPress.com that includes:

- Login protection
- Spam filtering
- Downtime monitoring
- Basic analytics
- Optional backups and image optimization

Jetpack sometimes overlaps with other plugins, so if you use it, only activate the modules you really need. Keeping your plugin list short will keep your site faster and reduce conflicts.

Additional security tips:

- Never use "admin" as your username.
- Set strong passwords and enable two-factor authentication if possible.
- Keep WordPress, themes, and plugins **updated**.
- Install a dedicated security plugin like **Wordfence** or **iThemes Security** if you want more detailed control.

Speed and Performance Tips

As your site grows, you'll add pages, images, and features. To keep things fast:

- Use **caching** (your host may include it, or use a plugin like WP Super Cache).
- Compress images before upload.
- Delete unused plugins and themes.
- Test your site speed regularly at **GTmetrix.com** or **PageSpeed Insights**.

Remember: visitors expect pages to load in **under three seconds** — especially on mobile.

Simple Exercise: Build and Test a Page

1. Create a new page titled "Contact Us."
2. Add a heading block, short paragraph, and contact form (using WPForms).
3. Insert a Google Map block or iframe showing your location.
4. Test it on your phone — does it load fast, look clean, and send emails correctly?

Once that works, you've mastered the basic workflow.
You can duplicate this process for any page — Home, About, Services, or Blog — using the same building blocks.

Final Thoughts

Building pages in WordPress is where your website finally takes shape.

With today's tools, you don't need to code — you just need structure, consistency, and good judgment about which plugins truly add value.

Elementor, Otter, Jetpack, WPForms — they're all useful in the right situations.

But remember, simpler is faster. Keep your site lean, secure, and mobile-friendly, and your visitors will thank you with clicks, calls, and sales.

Your website is now alive. From here forward, your focus shifts to growing its visibility — and that begins with mastering SEO and ongoing optimization.

PART IV – VISIBILITY: SEO, ANALYTICS & MARKETING

Chapter 12 – Understanding SEO

If you've ever wondered why some websites show up first in Google while others don't appear until page five, the answer is three letters that control everything: **SEO.**

Search Engine Optimization is both art and science — the practice of making your website easy for search engines to find, understand, and recommend. It's how you turn an invisible website into one that gets traffic day after day without paying for ads.

Most people think SEO is a mystery known only to experts. It isn't. You don't need expensive tools or technical degrees — just an understanding of what search engines look for and how to speak their language.

How Search Engines Rank Sites

Search engines like Google use automated programs called **crawlers** (or spiders) to scan the internet and index content. When someone searches for "handcrafted furniture," Google looks through billions of pages to find which ones:

1. Match the words in the query (relevance),
2. Provide helpful, high-quality content (authority), and
3. Load fast, look good on mobile, and are safe (usability).

Google then sorts those pages based on hundreds of ranking factors — everything from keyword use and backlinks to security, page speed, and freshness of content.

Think of it like this:

Google's job is to **recommend** the best possible answer to every question.

Your job is to make your website the most **reliable and relevant** answer.

Keyword Research Fundamentals

Keywords are the backbone of SEO — they're the exact words people type into search bars to find what they need.

But keyword research isn't about stuffing your site with repeated phrases. It's about understanding *your customers' intent.*

There are three basic keyword types:

1. **Informational:** "How to refinish a mahogany desk"
2. **Navigational:** "Glenn Website Design contact"
3. **Transactional:** "Buy handmade furniture online"

Each page of your website should focus on one main keyword or phrase — plus a few variations.

Where to Find the Right Keywords

The best free tool is **Google Keyword Planner**, part of Google Ads. You'll need to create an account, but using it for research is completely free.

Here's how to use it:

- Enter a few phrases that describe your business.
- The tool will show monthly search volumes, competition levels, and related ideas.
- Look for keywords that have good search volume but aren't overly competitive.

Other helpful (and free) tools include:

- **Ubersuggest** (by Neil Patel)
- **AnswerThePublic** – great for question-based keywords.
- **Google Search Console** – shows which searches are already bringing traffic to your site.

The key is to find keywords that reflect what *your customers* actually type, not what you *think* they type.

On-Page Optimization

On-page SEO means everything you do **within your own website** to help it rank higher.
Here are the most important elements and how to optimize each one.

1. Titles

Each page should have a unique, descriptive title (the text that appears in browser tabs and search results).
Example:

✅ *Custom Mahogany Furniture | Glenn Website Design*
Avoid vague titles like "Home" or "Welcome."

2. Meta Descriptions

This is the short summary below your link on Google.
Write it like an ad — clear, honest, and inviting.
Keep it under 160 characters and include your main keyword naturally.
Example:
Handcrafted mahogany furniture made to order. Shop desks, cabinets, and tables built to last a lifetime.

3. Headings (H1, H2, H3)

Use heading tags to organize your content.

- **H1:** Page title (only one per page)
- **H2s and H3s:** Subtopics or supporting ideas
  Include your keyword in at least one heading.

4. Internal Links

Link to other relevant pages on your site.
For example, a "Custom Desks" page should link to your "About" page and "Contact" form.
This helps visitors explore — and helps Google understand how your pages relate.

5. Image Alt Text

Add short descriptive text for every image.
Example: *Close-up of handmade Tiffany table lamp.*

6. Page Speed & Mobile Optimization

Google ranks faster, mobile-friendly pages higher.
Compress your images, use caching plugins, and test your site at https://pagespeed.web.dev.

Off-Page Signals and Backlinks

Off-page SEO happens *outside* your website — mostly through **links** and **reputation**.

A **backlink** is when another site links to yours. Google sees it as a "vote of confidence."
The more trusted sites that link to you, the higher your authority.

Good backlinks come from:

- Industry directories
- Guest blog posts
- Mentions in news articles
- Partner or client websites

Bad backlinks (from spammy or unrelated sites) can hurt your ranking.

Never buy links — Google is smarter than that.
Earn them through useful, shareable content instead.

Other off-page signals include:

- Consistent **business listings** (Google Maps, Yelp, directories)
- Positive **reviews**
- **Social media engagement** — while not a direct ranking factor, it increases visibility and clicks.

SEO Plugins and Tools

WordPress makes SEO much easier through plugins that automate the technical details.
Two of the best are **Yoast SEO** and **Rank Math**.

Yoast SEO

- Great for beginners.
- Helps you optimize titles, meta descriptions, and readability.
- Automatically generates XML sitemaps.

Rank Math

- A bit more advanced, with built-in schema markup and analytics integration.
- Excellent for multiple sites or deeper control.

Both are free with paid upgrades. I use **Yoast** on simpler sites and **Rank Math** on larger ones that need more precision.

Schema Markup: Helping Google Understand You

Schema is structured data that tells search engines exactly what's on your page — products, prices, reviews, events, or FAQs.

You've seen this in action when a search result shows star ratings, product images, or prices directly in Google. That's schema.

Plugins like **Rank Math** and **Yoast** add schema automatically, but you can also use **Google's Structured Data Markup Helper** to build it manually.

Schema doesn't guarantee a ranking boost, but it increases visibility and makes your listings look professional and trustworthy.

Simple Exercise: Check and Tune Your SEO

1. Choose one page of your website.
2. Open it in your SEO plugin.
3. Write a clear title and meta description.
4. Add your keyword in the first paragraph, one subheading, and the image alt tags.
5. Test it using **Google Search Console** after publishing.

This simple process — done consistently — will build a solid SEO foundation across your site.

Final Thoughts

SEO isn't a one-time task. It's a habit — small, consistent improvements that compound over time.

Don't chase algorithms or shortcuts.
Instead, focus on three timeless rules:

1. Create helpful, original content.

2. Use clear, descriptive language.

3. Build real trust online and offline.

When you do, Google will eventually reward you — not because you tricked it, but because you helped it do its job:

connecting people with what they're truly looking for.

Chapter 13 – Studying Your Competition

Once your website is live and optimized, the next question is: **"How do I get ahead of everyone else doing the same thing?"**

The answer lies in **competitive analysis** — understanding what others in your field are doing right, learning from it, and then doing it better.

You're not trying to copy competitors; you're studying their patterns, keywords, backlinks, and designs to uncover opportunities they've missed. This is where smart website owners separate themselves from the rest.

Why Competitor Analysis Matters

When you open a business in the real world, you look at who's across the street — their prices, their signage, their service. Online, the same principle applies — only now your competitors aren't across town; they're across the planet.

Analyzing competitors helps you:

- See what keywords and phrases bring them traffic.
- Understand which of their pages perform best.
- Identify gaps in their content or services.
- Benchmark design, usability, and overall user engagement.

Think of it as **digital reconnaissance.**
You're gathering intelligence before improving your own strategy.

Tools for Analyzing Top Competitors

You don't have to guess what works — there are plenty of free and paid tools that show real data.

Here are some I recommend:

1. Google Search

Start simple. Type your main keywords into Google and note which businesses appear on the first page.
Those are your top competitors. Study their titles, descriptions, and design styles.

2. Google Keyword Planner

You've already used this for your own keyword research. Now use it to discover which terms your competitors rank for — and how much search volume those words have.

3. Ubersuggest (Neil Patel)

Shows keyword rankings, estimated traffic, and even backlink data for any website.
Enter your competitor's domain and see which pages bring them the most visitors.

4. SimilarWeb

Great for estimating monthly traffic, visitor sources, and engagement metrics.
It helps you see where their audience comes from — search, social media, or referrals.

5. Ahrefs or SEMrush

Paid tools, but incredibly powerful.
They show backlink profiles (who links to them), keyword gaps, and technical SEO comparisons.
Even using the free versions gives you valuable insight.

6. Google Business Profile

Search your competitor's name on Google Maps.
Look at their reviews, photos, and posting frequency.
A well-maintained profile often drives as much traffic as the website itself.

Keyword Gap and Content Gap Analysis

A **keyword gap** is what your competitors rank for that you don't. A **content gap** is when they have pages or topics you haven't covered yet — or when their information is outdated, and you can do it better.

Here's a simple process:

1. Make a list of your top three competitors.
2. Enter each into Ubersuggest or Ahrefs and export their top-ranking keywords.
3. Compare them with your own keyword list.
4. Highlight any keywords you don't currently target.
5. Check their content — can you write something more detailed, current, or visual?

This approach gives you a ready-made roadmap of what to create next.

It's smarter than guessing — you're building based on proven interest.

Benchmarking Design, Performance, and Engagement

Competitor analysis isn't just about words — it's also about *presentation and experience.*

When studying other sites, ask:

- **Design:** Is their layout clean and modern? How's their use of color, spacing, and visuals?
- **Performance:** Do their pages load quickly? Use https://gtmetrix.com to compare.
- **Engagement:** How easy is it to find information or take action?
- **Trust:** Do they show testimonials, real photos, or certifications?
- **Mobile Experience:** How does their site perform on a phone?

Benchmarking doesn't mean copying. It means identifying the standards of your industry and finding ways to raise them.

Example:
If all your competitors have plain photo galleries, consider adding short videos or 360° views.
If their blogs are thin, publish deep guides with visuals.
If their contact forms are buried, make yours prominent and fast.

Every small improvement is a competitive edge.

Turning Insights into Advantage

Once you've analyzed your competitors, it's time to put that knowledge to work.

Here's how to turn research into real results:

1. **Find their strengths — then match or exceed them.**
   If they're ranking high for "custom furniture," study how they use that keyword in titles and headings, then create your own version that's richer in detail and value.

2. **Find their weaknesses — then fill the gap.**
   If they have slow loading times or outdated blog posts, build content that's faster, fresher, and more helpful.

3. **Update your design and usability.**
   Keep improving. Modern design signals a modern business.

4. **Strengthen your Google Business Profile.**
   Add photos, post updates, and reply to reviews — every one of those actions helps your visibility.

5. **Monitor results.**
   Use **Google Search Console** to track which keywords are improving.
   Over time, you'll see which strategies are paying off.

Remember: your goal isn't just to "beat competitors." It's to make your website *the better experience* — for both users and search engines.

Expanding into Marketing: Getting Eyes on Your Site

Once you've analyzed and improved your foundation, it's time to **market your website** — the bridge between good SEO and real-world traffic.

1. Social Media

Choose platforms where your audience actually spends time.
For visual products, focus on Instagram and Pinterest.
For professional services, LinkedIn or Facebook might work better.

Post consistently, link back to your site, and use real photos — not canned content.

2. Google Business Profile

This free listing is critical for local visibility.
Update your business hours, respond to reviews, and post photos regularly.

When customers search "near me," this is often the first thing they see — even before your website.

3. Email Lists

Your website should collect email addresses through forms or pop-ups.

Offer something of value — a free guide, a discount, or insider updates.

Use email to share new products, blogs, or seasonal promotions.

Email may not be flashy, but it remains one of the **highest converting marketing channels** on the internet.

4. Ad Campaigns

If you want faster results, consider targeted ads.

- **Google Ads** reach people actively searching for your keywords.

- **Facebook and Instagram Ads** build awareness through visuals.

- **YouTube Ads** work well for storytelling and brand trust.

Set a small budget, test multiple variations, and watch which ads drive actual engagement — not just clicks.

Simple Exercise: Spy and Strategize

1. Pick your top two competitors.
2. Visit their sites and write down:
   - Their main keywords
   - The feel of their design
   - The types of content they publish
   - How easy it is to contact them
3. Then ask:
   - What do they do better than me?
   - What do they *miss* that I could do better?

This one-hour exercise often sparks new ideas faster than any SEO course.

Final Thoughts

Competition online is fierce — but also fair. The tools to research, compare, and improve are available to everyone. Those who use them consistently will always stay one step ahead.

Don't think of competitors as enemies; think of them as teachers. They've already done the testing for you — you just need to learn from it and raise the standard.

Your website doesn't need to be the loudest voice — just the **clearest, most useful, and most trustworthy** one in the room. Do that, and both people and search engines will notice.

Chapter 14 –AI and Trends for Keyword Research

Search habits evolve constantly. What people type today may vanish from Google's radar next month. That's why keyword research is not a one-time setup — it's an ongoing process that blends creativity, data, and awareness of cultural shifts.

The tools are better than ever, especially with the arrival of AI-driven assistants that can surface new opportunities faster than human brainstorming ever could.

This chapter will show you how to combine **AI**, **Google Trends**, and **real-world feedback** to build a keyword strategy that adapts as the market changes.

How to Use AI Tools for Topic Discovery

AI tools like **ChatGPT**, **Gemini**, and **Claude** can save you hours of manual brainstorming. They're great for discovering emerging questions, generating related topics, and even organizing keywords by intent.

You can ask AI to:

- Suggest trending blog topics or YouTube titles for your niche.
- Expand one keyword into 20 subtopics.
- Group keywords into intent types (buying, learning, comparing).
- Rewrite headlines for better click appeal.

Example prompts:

- "List 15 article ideas about eco-friendly interior design that people are likely searching for in 2025."
- "Give me keyword clusters related to 'home office furniture' with buying intent."

AI gives you ideas quickly — but remember, it's not a replacement for real search data. Always cross-check your findings with tools like **Google Keyword Planner**, **Ubersuggest**, or **AnswerThePublic** to confirm that people are *actually searching* those terms.

Pro Tip:
Create a shared spreadsheet for your keyword ideas. Track columns for:

- Keyword or topic
- Monthly search volume
- Competition level
- Content type (blog, video, landing page)
- Status (planned, in progress, published)

Over time, you'll build a living "idea bank" that reflects both AI suggestions and real-world validation.

Google Trends, AnswerThePublic, and Reddit Analysis

Each of these tools gives you a different angle on what people are talking about — and how those interests shift over time.

Google Trends

Google Trends shows the rise and fall of search interest for any keyword.
Use it to:

- Identify **seasonal spikes** (for example, "patio furniture" peaks every spring).
- Compare keyword strength (e.g., "AI web design" vs. "automated website builder").
- Find **breakout terms** — new phrases suddenly gaining traction.

HOW TO WEBSITE DESIGN

Plan content **before** the spike. If a topic climbs every March, publish in February.

AnswerThePublic

This tool turns a keyword into a web of real questions.
Type "SEO for beginners," and you'll see questions like:

- "What is SEO and how does it work?"

- "Is SEO worth it for small business?"
  Each of those questions can become its own article, video, or FAQ entry.
  The visual layout also helps you identify which question patterns keep repeating across topics.

Reddit, Quora, and Online Communities

Real people, real language, real frustration — that's what you'll find here.
Search communities related to your field and note what people ask, complain about, or share.
A Reddit thread titled *"Why is my WordPress site so slow?"* tells you that hundreds of people want an answer.
That's a content opportunity.

These forums also reveal *how people phrase things* — perfect for writing conversational SEO content that matches natural search intent.

Seasonal and Emerging Trend Mapping

Trends aren't random — they follow cycles. Some repeat yearly, some are triggered by events, and others rise unexpectedly because of technology or social change.

Use **Google Trends** or **Exploding Topics** to spot new patterns.
Make a simple chart with three categories:

1. **Evergreen keywords** – Always relevant (e.g., "web design tips")

2. **Seasonal keywords** – Predictable peaks (e.g., "holiday website offers")

3. **Emerging keywords** – Recently rising interest (e.g., "AI SEO tools")

For each, plan when to create or update content.

- Publish **before** seasonal peaks.
- Keep evergreen content updated yearly.
- React fast to emerging trends — timing is everything.

Example:
If "AI logo maker" starts trending, write an article or video titled *"Testing the Top AI Logo Makers — What Actually Works?"* before everyone else floods that topic.

Building an Editorial Calendar

Once you've collected your keywords and identified trends, organize everything into a content calendar.

Your **editorial calendar** should include:

- The topic or keyword.
- The content format (blog, video, infographic, product page).
- The target audience or intent.
- The planned publish date.
- The promotion method (social, email, paid ad).

You can build one easily using **Google Sheets**, **Trello**, or **Notion**.

Color-code by type:

- Blue for blogs
- Green for videos
- Yellow for tutorials
- Red for promotions

Best practice: Review your calendar monthly to adjust for performance, trends, or product launches. Flexibility is key.

Performance Checks, Updates, Analytics, and Content Refresh Strategies

Keyword research doesn't end when you publish your content — that's just the beginning.

To stay relevant, you need to **measure results**, **update regularly**, and **refine your strategy** based on data.

1. Performance Checks

Use tools like:

- **Google Search Console** – See which queries your pages are appearing for.
- **Google Analytics** – Track engagement, bounce rate, and conversions.
- **Ubersuggest / Ahrefs** – Monitor ranking changes for your target keywords.

Review your performance every month. If a post ranks on page two, look at how you can improve it — maybe update the intro, add visuals, or expand answers to key questions.

2. Updates and Optimization

Every few months, revisit your top-performing pages.

- Refresh outdated info.
- Add internal links to newer pages.
- Recheck titles and meta descriptions for accuracy.
- Compress large images and re-test page speed.

Google loves **freshness** — even small updates can boost rankings.

3. Analytics and Trend Alignment

Watch which topics rise or fade.

If one keyword drops in traffic but a related one grows, shift your focus.

This is how your SEO strategy evolves alongside your audience.

For example, if "AI web builder" begins outperforming "AI website generator," pivot your content accordingly.

4. Content Refresh Strategy

Plan an annual "content audit."
List every major page and mark:

- Needs rewrite

- Needs update

- Still performing well

Delete outdated posts that bring no traffic. It's better to have 20 active, high-quality pages than 200 forgotten ones.

Final Thoughts

AI and data tools are incredible — but they're just assistants. The real success comes from using what they reveal and combining it with your own insight and timing.

When you blend AI discovery with real search data, community feedback, and continuous analysis, your website becomes *alive* — learning, adapting, and improving with the market.

That's how you stop chasing trends and start *predicting them.*

Chapter 15 – Blogging and Content Marketing

If your website is your storefront, your **blog** is your voice. It's how you stay in front of your audience, share insights, and build authority.

Blogging isn't just about writing articles — it's about creating consistent, valuable content that keeps people (and search engines) coming back.

Done right, a blog becomes your most powerful marketing tool. It attracts new visitors through search, gives returning readers a reason to stay, and turns casual browsers into loyal customers.

How Blogs Drive Traffic and Credibility

A blog is your chance to teach, share, and demonstrate expertise. When people search for solutions, your posts can be what they find first. Each blog post acts like a new "door" into your website — the more doors you have, the more visitors walk in.

Benefits of maintaining a blog include:

- **Organic traffic growth:** Every post is another opportunity to rank on Google.
- **Authority building:** Sharing real advice positions you as an expert.
- **Customer trust:** Helpful content builds credibility faster than ads ever could.
- **Conversion support:** Readers who trust your content are far more likely to buy.

Blogs work quietly but powerfully. While social media posts disappear within days, a good blog article can bring visitors for years.

Tip: Think of your blog as your digital handshake — it's often the first interaction people have with your brand.

Writing Evergreen vs. Trending Posts

There are two main types of blog content, and a strong content strategy includes both.

1. Evergreen Content

These are posts that stay relevant year after year — "evergreen" because they never go out of season.
Examples:

- "How to Choose the Right Web Host for Your Business"
- "Beginner's Guide to SEO"
- "What Every Website Needs Before Launch"

Evergreen posts build a foundation of steady, long-term traffic. They're perfect for tutorials, guides, and educational content.

2. Trending Content

These posts tap into current conversations, technologies, or news.
Examples:

- "How AI Is Changing Web Design in 2025"
- "The New Google Update and What It Means for Small Business Websites"

Trending posts attract spikes of traffic quickly — great for brand visibility and social shares.
Even though trends fade, they often bring new visitors who later explore your evergreen content.

Best Strategy:
Balance both. Use evergreen posts for stability and trending ones for momentum.

Building Content Pillars

A content pillar is a major topic that supports multiple related posts.

For example, if your website is about **web design**, your pillars might be:

1. SEO Basics

2. WordPress Tutorials

3. Design Trends

4. Website Maintenance

Each pillar acts as a "hub," linking to smaller related posts ("spokes") that explore subtopics in depth.

This structure not only helps readers navigate easily but also tells Google your site has *authority* in those areas.

Example:

Your pillar page might be *"The Ultimate Guide to WordPress."* Supporting posts could include:

- "How to Choose a WordPress Theme"

- "Best Plugins for Small Business Websites"

- "Fixing Common WordPress Errors"

All link back to the main pillar page — creating a web of internal links that boosts SEO and reader engagement.

Editorial Calendars for Consistency

Consistency is what separates a real content strategy from random posting.

An **editorial calendar** helps you plan topics, schedule publishing dates, and maintain momentum.

Your calendar should include:

- Post title or topic

- Target keyword or goal

- Author or responsible person

- Draft date and publish date

- Promotion method (social, email, ad)

You can use **Google Sheets**, **Trello**, or **Notion** to manage it. Aim for at least one new post per month if you're a small business — weekly if you want faster growth.

Tip:
Use AI tools or your keyword research from Chapter 14 to fill future topics. That way, your content stays aligned with real search trends.

Guest Posting, Collaborations, and Link-Building

Once your blog has a few solid posts, it's time to expand your reach through collaboration.

Guest Posting

Offer to write posts for other websites in your niche.
In return, include a short bio and a link back to your site.
This builds backlinks — one of the strongest signals Google uses to judge credibility — and exposes you to a new audience.

Collaborations

Partner with related businesses or creators.
Examples:

- A photographer writing a guest article on your design blog.
- A furniture company featuring your interior design advice.
- A teacher linking your English course from their education site.

Collaboration creates fresh, authentic cross-promotion that benefits everyone.

Link-Building

Links are like votes of confidence from the web. The best backlinks come naturally from useful, shareable content — guides, checklists, and research posts.
Avoid buying links or joining link farms; Google penalizes that instantly.

Converting Readers into Customers

Traffic is nice. Sales are better.
Your blog should lead visitors toward taking real action.

Calls-to-Action (CTAs)

At the end of each post, include a clear next step:

- "Get a Free Quote"
- "Download the Guide"
- "See Our Portfolio"
- "Book a Consultation"

Make it easy for readers to connect with you the moment they're ready.

Lead Magnets

Offer something free — a checklist, mini-guide, or email series — in exchange for their email address.
This turns casual readers into long-term subscribers and gives you a direct way to nurture leads through email marketing.

Repurpose Your Content

Don't let a blog post live and die on your site.
Turn it into:

- A short video for YouTube or TikTok.
- A carousel post on LinkedIn or Instagram.
- A snippet for your email newsletter.

You've already done the hard work of creating the content — now make it travel.

Simple Exercise: 3-Post Launch Plan

If you're starting a new blog, begin with these three posts:

1. An evergreen "how-to" guide.
2. A personal or story-based post about your business journey.
3. A trend-focused article relevant this season.

This combination covers the three types of visitors — learners, explorers, and buyers — and gives Google a clear signal of your expertise.

Final Thoughts

Blogging isn't just about writing — it's about **building trust at scale.** Every post you publish becomes another connection point between you and your future customers.

Write with value, update regularly, and link everything together into a larger story about your brand. The more helpful and human your content feels, the more readers will come back — and eventually, become customers.

Your blog is your voice.
Use it to educate, to connect, and to remind the world why your business exists.

Chapter 16 – Local SEO, Google Business Profile, and Merchant Center

If your business serves a specific area or sells products locally, **local SEO** is your lifeline. It ensures that when people nearby search for what you offer, *your business appears first* — on Google Maps, in the "near me" results, and even in the Shopping tab.

This chapter connects all the pieces: optimizing your Google Business Profile, earning reviews, using local keywords, and — for product sellers — adding your listings to **Google Merchant Center** so they appear right inside Google's shopping results.

Setting Up Google Business

Your **Google Business Profile (GBP)** — formerly *Google My Business* — is your local visibility foundation.
It's how your company appears in Google Search and Maps when people look for products or services nearby.

How to Set It Up

1. Go to https://www.google.com/business.
2. Sign in with your Google account.
3. Enter your business name, category, and service area.
4. Add your contact info, hours, and website.
5. Verify ownership — usually by postcard, phone, or email.

After verification, complete every field you can:

- Add a logo, cover photo, and 5–10 high-quality pictures of your space or products.
- Write a business description using clear, local keywords ("Custom wood furniture in Tulsa, Oklahoma").
- Use the *Posts* feature weekly to announce updates, promotions, or new arrivals.

A fully completed and active profile signals credibility to both Google and your potential customers.

Getting Reviews and Citations

Reviews

Online reviews are the strongest ranking factor for local SEO. They build trust and directly influence how high you appear in map results.

Encourage reviews naturally:

- Ask customers right after a purchase or project completion.
- Include your Google review link in follow-up emails.
- Print a QR code on invoices or packaging that leads straight to your review page.

Always respond to reviews — good or bad — with professionalism. A polite, helpful reply shows future customers that you care about feedback.

Citations

Citations are listings of your **business name, address, and phone number (NAP)** on other websites.
Consistency is key. Make sure your NAP is *identical* across:

- Google Business Profile
- Facebook Business Page
- Yelp
- Bing Places
- Local directories or trade listings

Even small inconsistencies ("Rd." vs. "Road") can hurt your local ranking, so copy-and-paste your exact format everywhere.

Local Keyword Optimization

Local SEO means focusing on the phrases people in your region actually type.

Examples:

- "Mahogany furniture in Tulsa"
- "Website designer near Jakarta"
- "Best pizza delivery in Sanur"

Use these phrases naturally throughout:

- Homepage titles and meta descriptions
- Blog posts and service pages
- Image alt text ("Custom oak table built in Tulsa, OK")
- Google Business description and posts

If you serve multiple areas, create **dedicated location pages** with unique descriptions for each city or district.
This gives each page a chance to rank independently.

Google Merchant Center and Local Product Listings

If your business sells products (online or in-store), setting up **Google Merchant Center (GMC)** is the next step toward full visibility.
It connects your store's inventory with Google Shopping, Maps, and local results — so customers can see what you sell *before* they even visit.

Why It Matters

When shoppers search "buy Tiffany lamp near me" or "solid teak dining set," Google often shows product listings at the top or in Maps.
Those listings come directly from Merchant Center feeds linked to your website and Google Business Profile.

How to Set Up Merchant Center

1. Go to https://merchants.google.com.
2. Sign in with your Google account.

3. Add your business information and **verify your website domain.**

4. Create a **product feed** — a spreadsheet or plugin integration that includes:

    o Product title and ID

    o Description

    o Price and availability

    o Image URL

    o Link to your website product page

    o Local pickup or shipping details

5. Link your **Merchant Center** account to your **Google Business Profile.**

6. Configure tax and shipping rules.

7. Submit your feed for review.

Once approved, your products can appear in:

- The **Google Shopping** tab

- **Local inventory ads**

- **Google Maps product listings**

Optimization Tips

- Use local phrases in product titles (e.g., "Handcrafted teak chair – Made in Bali").

- Upload clear, high-resolution photos.

- Keep pricing consistent with your website.

- Enable "local pickup" for in-store customers.

- Regularly check for disapproved items in the Merchant Center dashboard.

Pro Tip:

If you're running a WooCommerce site, install a *Google Product Feed plugin* — it automates most of this process.

Mobile and Map Integration

Most local searches happen on smartphones.
Make sure your site is fast, mobile-friendly, and easy to navigate.

Checklist:

- Test your site on multiple screen sizes.
- Ensure your phone number is clickable (tel: link).
- Embed a **Google Map** on your Contact or Visit Us page.
- Display your business hours and directions clearly.
- Compress images to keep mobile load times under 3 seconds.

Voice search is also growing — people say things like *"Who sells custom desks near me?"*
Include conversational phrases and FAQ sections that answer those questions naturally.

Simple Exercise: Full Local Visibility Tune-Up

1. Search your business name on Google — see what appears.
2. Verify your Google Business Profile is complete and accurate.
3. Upload 10+ high-quality photos.
4. Ask three customers for new reviews this week.
5. Check your website for local keywords and mobile performance.
6. Set up or verify your **Google Merchant Center** and submit your product feed.
7. Test your store listing in both Search and Maps.

Final Thoughts

Local SEO is your bridge between the digital and physical world.

When you combine a strong Google Business presence with positive reviews, optimized local keywords, and Merchant Center listings, your business can dominate both search results and shopping visibility.

It's not about reaching everyone — it's about being found *exactly where your best customers are looking.*

Make Google your storefront window.
Keep it clean, current, and shining bright for the locals passing by online.

Chapter 17 – Analytics and Conversion Tracking

Once your website is live, optimized, and bringing in visitors, the next big question is:

"What's actually working?"

You can't improve what you don't measure.
That's where analytics and conversion tracking come in — giving you the numbers behind your traffic, sales, and engagement.

This chapter explains how to install and use **Google Analytics**, **Search Console**, and other tools like **heatmaps** to understand visitor behavior and make smarter decisions that increase results over time.

Installing Google Analytics and Search Console

The two tools every serious website owner needs are **Google Analytics 4 (GA4)** and **Google Search Console**.
Together, they show you *who's visiting*, *what they're doing*, and *how they found you.*

Google Analytics (GA4)

Tracks:

- How many people visit your site.
- Which pages they view.
- How long they stay.
- Where they come from (Google, Facebook, direct, etc.).
- What actions they take (contact forms, purchases, downloads).

How to Install:

1. Visit https://analytics.google.com and sign in.
2. Click **Admin → Create Property → Web.**
3. Add your website name and URL.
4. Copy the tracking code provided.
5. Paste it into your WordPress site using a plugin such as **GA Google Analytics** or directly in your theme's header file.

Pro Tip:

If you use Rank Math or Yoast SEO, they include integration options for Analytics and Search Console — no extra code required.

Google Search Console

Monitors:

- How your pages perform in Google Search.
- Which keywords bring clicks.
- Errors or indexing issues.
- Backlinks to your site.

How to Set Up:

1. Visit https://search.google.com/search-console.
2. Add your domain (not just the URL prefix).
3. Verify ownership (use the same Google account as Analytics).
4. Wait a few days for data to appear.

This pairing — Analytics + Search Console — gives you both sides of the story: *traffic behavior* and *search visibility.*

Reading Key Metrics

Numbers are meaningless unless you know what they represent.

Here are the most important metrics to track — and what they actually mean.

1. Bounce Rate

The percentage of visitors who leave your site after viewing only one page.

A high bounce rate (over 70%) means visitors aren't finding what they expected — or your page loads too slowly.

Fix it by:

- Improving content clarity.
- Speeding up load times.
- Adding internal links or "next step" CTAs.

2. CTR (Click-Through Rate)

From Google Search Console, this shows how many people clicked your listing after seeing it.

Low CTR = your title or description needs improvement.

Fix it by:

- Writing more specific, benefit-driven titles.
- Using action words like "Discover," "Shop," or "Learn."
- Adding your location or value point (e.g., "Custom Desks – Made in Tulsa").

3. Conversion Rate

The percentage of visitors who complete your desired action — whether it's a purchase, signup, or contact form submission. You can set up conversion goals directly in GA4.

Fix it by:

- Simplifying your forms.
- Using stronger CTAs.
- Ensuring mobile checkout is easy.

4. Average Session Duration

Shows how long people spend on your site.
Short times can mean your content isn't engaging — or it's just too short.

Fix it by:

- Adding images, videos, and clear headings.
- Writing content that answers real questions fully.

5. Traffic Sources

Found in GA4 under *Acquisition → Overview.*
Shows where visitors come from:

- **Organic Search** (Google)
- **Direct** (typed your URL manually)
- **Social** (Facebook, Instagram, etc.)
- **Referral** (links from other sites)

This tells you which marketing channels deserve more attention — and which need improvement.

Setting Goals and Funnels

Analytics becomes powerful when you track what actually matters.

That's where **goals** and **funnels** come in.

Goals

A goal is any measurable action that benefits your business, such as:

- A form submission.
- A purchase.
- A download.
- A phone click (on mobile).

In GA4, you can define these under **Events** and mark them as conversions.

Funnels

A funnel tracks the *steps* people take before completing a goal.

Example:

Homepage → Product Page → Cart → Checkout → Purchase

By studying your funnel, you can see *where* visitors drop off. Maybe your cart page loads too slowly, or your checkout form asks for too much information.

Fixing those weak spots can double your conversions without spending another cent on ads.

Pro Tip:

Start small. Track one simple conversion first — like a contact form submission — then expand to purchases and other actions.

Using Data to Improve Performance

Once your analytics are running, treat the data like a teacher. Don't check numbers for curiosity — check them for *clues.*

1. Identify Top Performers

Find your most visited and highest-converting pages.
Ask: What's working here? Can I duplicate this format elsewhere?

2. Improve Underperforming Pages

Pages with high impressions but low clicks may need better titles or meta descriptions.
Pages with good traffic but low conversions might need stronger CTAs.

3. Watch for Traffic Patterns

Is traffic spiking after certain blog posts or ads?
Do weekends perform better than weekdays?
Timing matters — use those patterns to plan your promotions.

4. Add Heatmaps

Tools like **Hotjar** or **Microsoft Clarity** show where users click, scroll, and stop reading.
They reveal how people actually interact with your layout.
If most clicks miss your CTA button, maybe it's placed too low or blends into the background.

5. Keep Adjusting

Analytics isn't a one-time project — it's an ongoing conversation between you and your visitors.
Every few months, use your findings to tweak design, update content, or refine your keyword targeting.

Simple Exercise: Your First Conversion Funnel

1. Open Google Analytics → Admin → Events.
2. Mark "form_submit" or "purchase_complete" as a conversion.
3. Wait a week for data.
4. Look at the user flow (path visitors take before converting).
5. Identify one bottleneck and test a fix — such as a shorter form or clearer button.

Even small adjustments based on data can make a huge difference in sales.

Final Thoughts

Numbers don't lie — but they also don't speak unless you know how to listen. Google Analytics, Search Console, and heatmaps are your translator.

By understanding what the data tells you, you'll know *what to fix, what to repeat, and what to stop doing altogether.*

Design attracts attention. SEO brings traffic.
But analytics turns visitors into customers — and customers into long-term success.

PART V – MONETIZATION & GROWTH

Chapter 18 – Turning Traffic into Income

You've built your website, optimized it for search, and started seeing real visitors. Now comes the fun part — turning that traffic into income.

Whether you're selling physical products, digital downloads, services, or ad space, your website can become a full-time business. This chapter covers the major monetization models — from e-commerce to affiliate links — and walks you through setting up systems that make money even when you're not online.

Selling Products with WooCommerce

If your goal is to sell products directly from your website, **WooCommerce** is the go-to solution for WordPress. It's free, flexible, and integrates with nearly every major payment processor.

Installing WooCommerce

1. Go to your WordPress Dashboard → *Plugins* → *Add New*.
2. Search for **WooCommerce**, install, and activate.
3. Follow the Setup Wizard to configure:
   - Store details (address, currency, preferred units).
   - Product type (physical, digital, or both).
   - Payment methods (PayPal, Stripe, credit cards).
   - Shipping settings.

WooCommerce automatically adds essential pages:

- **Shop** – Displays all products.
- **Cart** – Shows selected items.

123

- **Checkout** – Handles payments.
- **My Account** – Allows customers to track orders.

Adding Products

1. Go to *Products → Add New.*
2. Add a title, description, price, and at least one high-quality image.
3. Choose the product type:
    - **Simple Product** – One item with one price.
    - **Variable Product** – Different sizes, colors, or options.
    - **Downloadable Product** – Digital goods like e-books, photos, or lessons.
4. Set stock levels and shipping weights if applicable.

Optimizing Product Pages

- Use descriptive titles with relevant keywords.
- Write genuine, benefit-driven product descriptions.
- Add multiple images and short demo videos.
- Include customer reviews and trust badges (SSL, money-back guarantees).

Integrating Payment Gateways

WooCommerce supports most major gateways:

- **Stripe** (credit/debit, Apple Pay, Google Pay)
- **PayPal**
- **Square**
- **Bank transfer or COD** (optional for local sales)

Make sure SSL is active on your site — it's mandatory for processing secure payments.

Service Bookings and Payment Gateways

If your business sells *time* rather than *things* — consulting, coaching, classes, or design — you can turn your website into a booking platform.

Recommended Plugins

- **Amelia** – Full-featured appointment booking system.
- **Bookly** – Easy to use, great for small businesses.
- **Simply Schedule Appointments** – Simple and integrates with Google Calendar.

Each plugin allows:

- Scheduling appointments or sessions.
- Accepting payments directly via Stripe or PayPal.
- Sending email confirmations and reminders.

Example:

A web designer can let clients schedule consultations right from the site, pay a deposit via Stripe, and automatically block that slot in Google Calendar — all without a single email exchange.

Affiliate Marketing and Ad Networks

If you don't have your own product, you can still earn income by promoting others' products or hosting ads on your site.

Affiliate Marketing

Affiliate programs pay you a commission when someone clicks your unique referral link and buys something.

How to Start:

1. Choose a niche aligned with your content (e.g., tools, tech, travel, design).
2. Join affiliate networks:

- o **Amazon Associates**
- o **ShareASale**
- o **CJ Affiliate**
- o **Impact**

3. Add affiliate links to blog posts, reviews, or resource pages.
4. Disclose your relationship (required by law):

"As an affiliate, I may earn commissions from qualifying purchases."

Pro Tip:
Don't overload pages with links — readers trust honest, useful recommendations far more than endless promotions.

Advertising Networks

If your site generates consistent traffic (1,000+ monthly visits), you can monetize with ads.

Options include:

- **Google AdSense** – The easiest starting point.
- **Ezoic** – Higher revenue once you have 10,000+ visits/month.
- **Mediavine** – Premium ads for larger traffic sites (50,000+ sessions).

Setup (AdSense example):

1. Apply at https://adsense.google.com.
2. Add the verification code to your website.
3. Create ad units (auto-ads recommended).
4. Monitor performance through your AdSense dashboard.

Tip:
Balance ads carefully — too many can slow your site or annoy visitors.

Subscription Models and Digital Downloads

Subscription models turn one-time visitors into recurring customers — the key to stable, predictable income.

Membership or Subscription Plugins

- **MemberPress** – Create paywalled content or online courses.
- **Paid Memberships Pro** – Flexible and integrates with Stripe or PayPal.
- **WooCommerce Subscriptions** – Ideal if you already sell products or services.

These systems can handle:

- Monthly or annual subscriptions.
- Access control for premium content.
- Automatic renewals and cancellations.

Digital Downloads

If you create digital goods — e-books, templates, software, or music — you can sell them automatically using:

- **Easy Digital Downloads (EDD)**
- **WooCommerce Downloadable Products**

Customers receive instant file access after payment — no manual delivery needed.

Examples of profitable digital content:

- Photography packs
- Website templates
- Lesson PDFs or audio courses
- Industry-specific guides

Pricing Strategy Basics

Whether you're selling a product, a service, or a subscription, your price sends a message.
It's not just about cost — it's about **perceived value**.

Guidelines

- Research competitors, but don't undercut yourself.
- Bundle related services or products to increase average order value.
- Offer **three pricing tiers** (basic, standard, premium) — most customers pick the middle one.
- Use limited-time discounts or free shipping to encourage quick decisions.

Psychology of Pricing

- Prices ending in **.99** feel cheaper.
- Showing a **"was" price** highlights savings.
- Offering a **"most popular"** badge on one plan guides choice.

Simple Exercise: Choose Your Monetization Path

Ask yourself:

1. Am I selling **products**, **services**, or **knowledge**?
2. Do I want **passive income** (ads, affiliates) or **active income** (sales, bookings)?
3. What problem am I solving — and how can I make that clear to buyers?

Then pick **one** model to focus on first. You can always expand later, but clarity beats complexity in the beginning.

Final Thoughts

Monetization isn't about luck — it's about structure.
When your website is built with a solid foundation, adding income streams becomes simple.

Whether through WooCommerce, affiliate programs, or digital subscriptions, your website can become more than just an online presence — it can become a business that grows even while you sleep.

Don't chase every monetization trend.
Build one reliable stream first — then scale from there.

Chapter 19 – Email Marketing & Lead Capture

A website without a mailing list is like a store with no guest book. Visitors might stop by once, love what they see, and then disappear forever.

Email marketing changes that. It gives you a direct, personal channel to stay in touch — no algorithms, no middlemen, no social-media noise. Done right, it's still one of the most effective marketing tools ever created.

This chapter shows you how to capture leads, build mailing lists, automate follow-ups, and write newsletters that people actually look forward to opening.

Setting Up Mailing Lists

You'll need an email marketing service to manage subscribers, automate sequences, and stay compliant with spam laws (like GDPR or CAN-SPAM).

Here are some of the most trusted options, each with its own strengths:

- **Mailchimp** — Ideal for beginners.
  Offers a free plan for up to 500 contacts, a simple drag-and-drop editor, and plenty of ready-made templates.

- **Brevo (formerly Sendinblue)** — Great for small business owners.
  Combines email and SMS marketing, includes automation tools, and works well for transactional emails.

- **MailerLite** — Perfect if you want something clean and affordable.
  Easy to use, includes landing page tools, and offers visual automation for follow-ups.

- **ConvertKit** — Designed for creators, writers, and educators.
  Focuses on audience segmentation, tag-based automations, and personalized workflows.

- **FluentCRM** or **Groundhogg** — Best for WordPress power users.
  These are self-hosted plugins that run entirely within your site, keeping control of your data and reducing monthly costs.

Steps to Start

1. Create an account on your chosen platform.
2. Import any existing customer list (with permission).
3. Create a **signup form** or **popup** using the platform's built-in tools.
4. Connect the form to your website (we'll cover integration shortly).
5. Design a **welcome email** that sends automatically when someone subscribes.

Pro Tip:

Start small. A focused, high-quality list of 100 engaged subscribers can outperform 10,000 random ones.

Lead Magnets & Newsletter Automation

People don't hand over their email for nothing — you have to give them a reason.
That reason is called a **lead magnet.**

Examples of Effective Lead Magnets

- A free PDF guide ("10 SEO Fixes You Can Do in a Day")
- A discount code or coupon
- A short video tutorial or webinar
- A free downloadable checklist or template
- A mini-email course spread over 3–5 days

HOW TO WEBSITE DESIGN

Your lead magnet should solve a *specific, immediate problem* for your ideal customer — not a generic one.

Once someone signs up, automation takes over.

Automation Sequence Basics

1. **Welcome Email:** Thank them and deliver the lead magnet.
2. **Follow-Up 1 (1–2 days later):** Offer extra value — maybe a tip or story.
3. **Follow-Up 2 (3–5 days later):** Introduce your product or service naturally.
4. **Newsletter Sequence:** Move them into your regular weekly or monthly list.

Most platforms let you build these flows visually using "if this → then that" logic.

Example:

If user downloads the Free Web Design Checklist → Send 3-email series on choosing themes → Offer consult call.

Automation lets you stay in touch with every new subscriber automatically — even while you sleep.

Writing Conversion-Friendly Emails

Your emails don't need to be long; they need to be *read*.

Keep Them Simple & Personal

- Use the subscriber's name when possible.
- Write like you're talking to one person, not a crowd.
- Stick to one topic per email.
- Use short paragraphs and clear calls to action (CTA).

Structure for Impact

1. **Subject Line:** The hook. Keep it under 50 characters.

Example: "3 Simple Fixes to Speed Up Your Website Today"

2. **Opening:** Relate to a pain point or story.

3. **Value:** Share a quick tip, resource, or insight.

4. **CTA:** One clear action — "Read the full guide," "Shop now," "Reply and ask."

What to Avoid

- Generic sales language ("Buy now before it's too late!")
- Over-designed emails that look like ads — plain-text often performs better.
- Sending too frequently — 1–2 emails per week is plenty for most businesses.

Tracking Performance

Check these key metrics inside your email dashboard:

- **Open Rate:** % of people who open the email (20–40% is healthy).
- **Click-Through Rate (CTR):** % who clicked your link (2–5% is good).
- **Unsubscribe Rate:** Under 1% means your content still fits your audience.

Integrating Signup Forms with WordPress

The goal is to make subscribing effortless.

Methods

- Use your email platform's **official plugin** (Mailchimp for WP, Fluent Forms, MailerLite WP integration).
- Add signup forms in:
  - Sidebar widgets
  - Blog post footers
  - Pop-ups or slide-ins (try *Popup Maker* or *ConvertBox*)

  - Checkout pages (WooCommerce integration)
- Connect via **API keys** or HTML embed code from your mail service.

Best Practices

- Keep the form short — just name + email.
- Add a clear headline: "Get Free Weekly Design Tips."
- Show social proof: "Join over 500 subscribers learning with us."
- Test different placements and offers to see which converts best.

Pro Tip:

Integrate your signup form with Google Analytics or Meta Pixel so you can track which traffic sources bring the most email signups.

Simple Exercise: Your First Automation

1. Choose an email service (Mailchimp or MailerLite recommended for beginners).
2. Create a lead magnet and upload it (PDF or video link).
3. Build a landing page with a signup form.
4. Write a 3-email welcome sequence.
5. Promote the lead magnet on your homepage and social media.

By the end of this exercise, you'll have a fully automated system that turns visitors into subscribers without manual work.

Final Thoughts

Email marketing isn't about collecting addresses — it's about building relationships. Every message you send is a conversation that builds trust and moves someone closer to becoming a customer.

Visitors come and go, but a subscriber stays in your circle. Nurture that connection, and your email list will become the most valuable asset your website owns.

Chapter 20 – Social Media Integration

Your website is your home base — but social media is where your audience lives. If you want consistent traffic, trust, and engagement, you need to connect your site to the platforms people use every day.

Social integration isn't just about adding buttons. It's about building a two-way bridge between your website and your social channels — so followers can find your site easily, and your visitors can follow or share your content with one click.

This chapter walks you through connecting your site to major social platforms, adding proof and sharing tools, automating posts, and tracking results.

Connecting Your Site to Social Platforms

Every major social network allows you to connect your business website in a way that builds both visibility and credibility.

Here's how to integrate each effectively.

Facebook

- Create a **Facebook Page** (not a personal profile).
- Add your website link and a clear "About" description.
- Install the **Meta Pixel** on your website — this tracks visitors and helps retarget ads later.
- Use plugins like **Smash Balloon Facebook Feed** or **Jetpack Social** to display your latest posts directly on your site.

Instagram

- Switch to a **Business or Creator account** for analytics and contact buttons.
- Add your website in your profile bio (and use Linktree or Beacons if you need multiple links).
- Use the same feed plugin (Smash Balloon also supports Instagram) to embed your photos or reels into your site's gallery or homepage.
- Keep image styles consistent with your website's color palette — visual continuity builds trust.

YouTube

- Create a branded channel with your logo and website link in the banner and description.
- Embed your videos directly into blog posts and product pages using the built-in WordPress block.
- Consider a "How To" or "Behind the Scenes" playlist to drive authority traffic back to your website.
- Add YouTube subscribe buttons on your site's sidebar or footer.

LinkedIn

- Ideal for B2B services, consultants, and professionals.
- Create a **Company Page** and link to your website.
- Share your blog posts as LinkedIn Articles to reach new audiences.
- Add a **LinkedIn Follow button** using official plugins or code snippets.

Pro Tip:

Use consistent branding (profile photos, color themes, taglines) across every platform. People should instantly recognize your business wherever they find you online.

Social Proof and Sharing Buttons

Social proof is the modern version of word-of-mouth. When people see your content being shared, liked, or commented on, they trust your brand more.

Add Sharing Buttons

Use plugins like **AddToAny**, **ShareThis**, or **Sassy Social Share** to add easy one-click share buttons on your:

- Blog posts
- Product pages
- Portfolio pieces

Position them where people naturally finish reading — usually at the top, bottom, or floating alongside the page.

Pro Tip:

Use share counts carefully. Seeing "1 share" on a new post can discourage clicks, so hide counters until you have a few.

Social Proof Elements

You can also embed:

- Testimonials from Facebook or Google Reviews.
- Instagram photo galleries of customers using your products.
- "Featured on" badges (if your brand has media mentions).
- Video testimonials or influencer collaborations.

This kind of real-world validation increases both credibility and conversion rates.

Scheduling and Cross-Posting Automation

Posting manually on every social platform is exhausting. Fortunately, there are automation tools that can schedule and cross-post content across channels — keeping your accounts active without burning you out.

Recommended Tools

- **Meta Business Suite (Facebook & Instagram)** – Free, built-in scheduler.
- **Buffer** – Schedule posts across multiple platforms.
- **Later** – Excellent for Instagram grid planning and reels.
- **Hootsuite** – Great for teams managing multiple brands.
- **SocialBee** – Lets you recycle evergreen content automatically.

How to Automate

1. Plan your weekly or monthly content calendar.
2. Create 3–5 reusable templates (quotes, tips, new products, blog promos).
3. Schedule posts to go out at peak times for your audience.
4. Use different wording per platform — casual on Facebook, concise on Twitter/X, professional on LinkedIn.

You can even connect WordPress directly to social media using **Jetpack Social** or **Uncanny Automator**, which automatically posts your new blog articles to selected platforms the moment they go live.

Pro Tip:
Don't "set and forget." Check your notifications and comments. Engagement is still personal — automation should assist, not replace, conversation.

Tracking Social Traffic with UTM Links

If you're serious about growth, you need to know **which social platforms actually bring visitors** and sales.
That's where **UTM links** come in.

What Are UTM Links?

UTM (Urchin Tracking Module) tags are small bits of text added to the end of a URL. They help Google Analytics track where your visitors came from.

Example:

https://glennwebsitedesign.com/?utm_source=facebook&utm_medium=social&utm_campaign=spring_sale

In this example:

- **utm_source** = facebook
- **utm_medium** = social
- **utm_campaign** = spring_sale

When someone clicks this link, Google Analytics logs exactly which campaign and platform brought them in.

How to Create UTM Links

Use Google's free tool: https://ga-dev-tools.web.app/ga4/campaign-url-builder/

Then share those UTM links in your:

- Facebook posts
- Instagram bios
- YouTube video descriptions
- LinkedIn updates

After a week or two, you can open **Google Analytics → Acquisition → Traffic Sources** and see which channels drive the most conversions.

Simple Exercise: Social Integration Setup

1. Link your website on every social platform you use.
2. Add social sharing buttons to your blog posts.
3. Embed one social feed (Facebook, Instagram, or YouTube) on your homepage or footer.
4. Create and test one UTM link for your next social post.
5. Review analytics next week to see which post performed best.

Final Thoughts

Social media is where conversations start, but your website is where they convert.
When you connect the two — and track what's working — you create a continuous loop of engagement, trust, and sales.

The key is consistency: show up regularly, keep your message authentic, and always invite followers back to your website — your digital home base.

Don't just post — connect.
Your audience isn't just scrolling; they're looking for you.

PART VI – MAINTENANCE, SECURITY & SCALING

Chapter 21 – Security and Backups

It doesn't matter how beautiful your website is — if it's not secure, it's at risk. Every day, tens of thousands of websites are attacked or infected with malware. And contrary to what many think, hackers don't target only large corporations. Small business sites are easier targets because they're often unprotected or neglected.

This chapter covers everything you need to know to keep your website safe — from updates and backups to malware prevention, SSL certificates, and what to do if your site ever gets hacked.

Plugin and Theme Updates

One of the simplest ways to protect your website is also one of the most overlooked: **keeping everything updated.**

Outdated plugins and themes are the number one cause of website hacks. Developers release updates to patch vulnerabilities — if you ignore them, you're leaving the door wide open.

Enable Auto-Updates

Go to your WordPress dashboard under **Plugins → Installed Plugins**, and click "Enable auto-updates" for all trusted plugins. Do the same for your theme and WordPress core.

This ensures you're always running the latest, most secure versions without logging in every week.

Create a Child Theme

Your **child theme** isn't a duplicate of your main theme — it's a lightweight overlay that contains only the specific files you don't want overwritten during updates.

A typical child theme includes just three key files:

- **header.php** – where you place tracking code for Google Analytics, AdSense, and Search Console verification.

- **functions.php** – for adding or modifying PHP functions without altering the main theme's files.

- **style.css** – for your own design adjustments such as colors, typography, or spacing.

When the parent theme updates, these child theme files remain untouched. This setup protects your custom integrations and code while still allowing your main theme to receive important security and performance updates.

If you're using themes like **Neve**, **Astra**, or **GeneratePress**, most include a one-click child theme generator or clear documentation for manual setup.

Pro Tip:
After major updates, always test your homepage and contact forms. It takes only a few seconds and can save you hours of debugging later.

Backups and Restore Points

Security isn't only about preventing attacks — it's about being ready when something goes wrong.

Even the most secure website can face issues: plugin conflicts, accidental deletions, or server crashes. That's why **backups** are non-negotiable.

Offline Backups — The Safest Option

There are many ways to back up your site, but I've found the easiest, cheapest, and most reliable is **an offline backup file**.

I personally use **All-in-One WP Migration** — the gold standard for WordPress backups and transfers, used by over 60 million websites worldwide, from small blogs to Fortune 500 companies.

I recently used it to migrate **30 websites in one week**, which should tell you how efficient and dependable it is.

How It Works

- Install the plugin from your WordPress dashboard.
- Go to *All-in-One WP Migration → Export*.
- Export your full site (database, media, themes, and plugins) into a single downloadable file.
- Store that file on an external hard drive or cloud storage like Google Drive.

If disaster strikes, you can restore the site in minutes.

Upgrade for Large Sites

If your site is large or you manage multiple websites, you'll want the **All-in-One WP Migration Unlimited Extension**.

This premium version bypasses hosting upload limits, PHP timeouts, and file size restrictions.
It also allows advanced features such as:

- Full server restores
- Reset hub for managing multiple sites
- Command-line (CLI) automation

At around **$69 per site**, it's one of the best investments you can make for peace of mind.

Pro Tip:
Keep **two** backups — one local and one offsite. It's the digital equivalent of not keeping all your eggs in one basket.

SSL, Firewalls, and Anti-Spam Measures

SSL Certificates

Every site today needs **SSL (Secure Socket Layer)** — the "https://" in your address bar.
Most hosting providers (like DreamHost, SiteGround, and Hostinger) include free SSL certificates through **Let's Encrypt**.

If your site still shows "Not Secure," contact your host to enable SSL immediately. SSL not only protects visitor data but also boosts SEO and builds user trust.

Firewalls

A firewall monitors and blocks suspicious traffic before it reaches your site.
For WordPress, top choices include:

- **Wordfence Security** – robust protection with login attempt monitoring.
- **Sucuri Firewall** – excellent malware prevention and cleanup tools.
- **Cloudflare** – adds both security and global CDN performance benefits.

Each helps block brute-force attacks, bots, and malicious scripts before they cause damage.

Anti-Spam Tools

Spam comments and fake form submissions are more than just annoying — they can clog your system and even carry malware.
Install:

- **Akismet Anti-Spam** (created by the WordPress team).
- **reCAPTCHA** for contact forms and login pages.

These tools silently filter junk traffic before it ever reaches you.

Recognizing Hacking Attempts

Even with strong defenses, knowing the **warning signs** of a breach can save your site.

Common Red Flags

- Your homepage redirects to another site.
- Strange pop-ups or ads appear that you didn't add.
- You can't log in to WordPress — "invalid username" errors.
- Search engines mark your site as unsafe.
- Unknown users, plugins, or files appear in your dashboard.

If any of these happen, don't panic — just act fast.

What to Do

1. **Disable your site** temporarily via your hosting control panel.
2. **Restore a clean backup** using All-in-One WP Migration or your host's backup tool.
3. **Change all passwords** — WordPress, FTP, hosting, and database.
4. **Run a malware scan** using Wordfence or Sucuri.
5. **Recheck your analytics and AdSense accounts** to ensure no suspicious scripts were injected.
6. **Bring the site back online** only after verifying it's completely clean.

If you're unsure, most hosts (including DreamHost) offer professional malware cleanup services for a reasonable one-time fee.

Simple Exercise: Quick Security Audit

Take 10 minutes and check the following:

1. Is SSL active and showing the padlock icon?
2. Are auto-updates enabled for all plugins and themes?
3. Have you made a full backup in the last 30 days?
4. Is a firewall or security plugin installed and active?
5. Do your contact forms use CAPTCHA or anti-spam filters?

If you answered "no" to any of these, start fixing those immediately.

Final Thoughts

Website security isn't about paranoia — it's about protection and peace of mind. The more care you put into updates, backups, and firewalls today, the less you'll ever have to worry about tomorrow.

Hope for the best, plan for the worst — and keep a clean backup handy. Your website is an investment of time, creativity, and trust.

Treat it with the same protection you'd give any valuable asset — because once it's safe, it can keep working for you 24 hours a day.

Chapter 22 – Speed Optimization

Your website can look amazing, have great content, and still fail — simply because it's **too slow**.

In the online world, speed is everything. A one-second delay in page load time can reduce conversions by 7% and increase bounce rates by 30%. People won't wait — and neither will Google.

This chapter shows you how to make your site lightning fast using caching, CDNs, code cleanup, and testing tools — so your visitors (and search engines) stay happy.

Why Speed Matters

Speed affects every part of your website's performance:

- **SEO:** Google ranks faster sites higher.
- **User experience:** Visitors stay longer on quick sites.
- **Conversions:** People are more likely to buy or contact you if the page loads instantly.
- **Mobile traffic:** On slow connections, even a few extra seconds can mean losing half your audience.

Simply put, your website's speed is the first impression it makes before anyone reads a single word.

Caching, CDNs, and Image Compression

Caching

Caching stores copies of your web pages so that when visitors return, the site loads instantly without rebuilding each page from scratch.

Recommended caching plugins:

- **WP Super Cache** – Simple, free, and effective.
- **W3 Total Cache** – More advanced; includes database, object, and browser caching.
- **LiteSpeed Cache** – Works especially well with LiteSpeed servers and offers built-in image optimization.

Once installed, these plugins handle most optimization automatically.

Enable **browser caching** and **page caching**, and test your results.

Pro Tip:

After major updates, clear your cache so visitors see the newest version of your pages.

CDNs (Content Delivery Networks)

A CDN stores copies of your website across multiple servers around the world.

When someone visits your site, they're served data from the nearest server — reducing load times dramatically.

Popular CDN options:

- **Cloudflare** – Free for most small sites; adds both speed and security.
- **Bunny.net** – Fast, affordable, and integrates easily with WordPress.
- **StackPath** – Great for e-commerce and international websites.

CDNs work especially well for image-heavy sites or those with global traffic.

Image Compression

Images are often the biggest source of slowdowns.
Each large, uncompressed image can add seconds to your load time.

Use these optimization plugins:

- **Smush** – Automatically compresses and resizes images during upload.
- **ShortPixel** – Offers strong compression with minimal quality loss.
- **Imagify** – Includes bulk optimization and WebP format conversion.

Also, size your images properly before uploading.
A 4000px-wide photo is overkill for a section that displays at 800px.

Pro Tip:
Use **WebP** format for modern browsers — it cuts file size by up to 70% without losing visual quality.

Minimizing Scripts and Database Cleanup

Even with caching and CDNs, bloated code can still slow your site down.

Minify and Combine Scripts

Minification removes unnecessary spaces, comments, and line breaks in your CSS and JavaScript files, making them smaller and faster to load.

Plugins that handle this automatically:

- **Autoptimize** – Minifies CSS, JS, and HTML.
- **Asset CleanUp** – Lets you disable unused scripts per page.
- **Fast Velocity Minify** – Combines and compresses scripts efficiently.

Clean Your Database

Over time, your database fills with old post revisions, spam comments, and temporary data.
Cleaning it improves performance and reduces server load.

Use plugins like:

- **WP-Optimize**
- **Advanced Database Cleaner**

These can remove hundreds of unnecessary entries in seconds — just remember to back up your site first.

Pro Tip:
Avoid using too many heavy plugins. Every plugin adds code. Keep your list lean and deactivate anything you no longer use.

Testing with GTmetrix and Google PageSpeed

You don't have to guess how fast your site is — you can measure it.

GTmetrix

Visit https://gtmetrix.com, enter your website URL, and run a test.
It gives you a performance grade, load time, and a detailed list of what's slowing your site down.
Look for "waterfall" charts — they show exactly which files or scripts are the bottlenecks.

Google PageSpeed Insights

Go to https://pagespeed.web.dev.
This free tool gives you both a **mobile** and **desktop** score, along with optimization suggestions.

Pay close attention to:

- **Largest Contentful Paint (LCP):** How quickly your main content appears.

- **First Input Delay (FID):** How soon users can interact.

- **Cumulative Layout Shift (CLS):** How stable the layout is as it loads.

Try to keep your scores above **80** on both mobile and desktop.

From Glenn Website Design October 2025

Pro Tip:
Don't chase a perfect 100. Real-world user experience matters more than lab scores.

Mobile Speed vs. Desktop Speed Differences

Most of today's traffic comes from smartphones.
A site that loads in 2 seconds on desktop might take 5–6 seconds on mobile because of slower connections or smaller processors.

Here's how to fix that:

1. **Use a responsive theme.** Most modern WordPress themes (like Neve, Astra, or GeneratePress) already handle this well.
2. **Prioritize above-the-fold content.** Make sure the first visible section loads first.
3. **Lazy-load images and videos.** This delays loading offscreen elements until the user scrolls down.
4. **Avoid popups on mobile.** They slow down load times and hurt SEO.
5. **Test on real devices.** Emulators don't always reflect actual speed.

Pro Tip:

If your mobile speed is still slow, try a lightweight theme like **Blocksy** or **Kadence** and limit plugins that inject heavy JavaScript.

Simple Exercise: Performance Tune-Up

1. Run a speed test using GTmetrix and PageSpeed Insights.
2. Install one caching plugin and one image optimization plugin.
3. Activate Cloudflare's free CDN.
4. Optimize your homepage images and re-test.
5. Track improvement weekly for one month.

You'll likely see speed gains of 50–80% just from these steps.

Final Thoughts

Speed isn't a luxury — it's part of professionalism.
A fast website signals quality, care, and reliability before visitors even read your content.

Optimization doesn't have to be complicated. With caching, CDNs, clean code, and regular testing, even a beginner can run a site that loads in under three seconds.

In web design, patience is short and competition is fast. The quicker your site loads, the longer your visitors — and your profits — will stay.

Chapter 23 – Routine Maintenance Checklist

Building your website is the easy part — keeping it performing at its best takes ongoing care. Just like a car or a business, your website runs smoothly when you follow a maintenance schedule.

Routine maintenance prevents small issues from turning into big problems. It keeps your site secure, up to date, and visible in search results.

This chapter provides a checklist you can use every month, quarter, and year to keep your site fast, healthy, and profitable.

Monthly Tasks

These are your "must-do" maintenance habits. Doing them regularly prevents nearly all major problems before they start.

1. Backups

- Run a fresh backup of your site (files + database).
- Store a copy offline or in cloud storage.
- Test one backup every few months to ensure it actually restores correctly.

Pro Tip:

Schedule automatic backups through your host or plugin like *All-in-One WP Migration* or *UpdraftPlus*, but still download at least one manual copy monthly.

2. Plugin and Theme Checks

- Log in to your WordPress dashboard and check for available updates.
- Apply all plugin, theme, and core updates.
- Remove any plugins you're no longer using.
- Review active plugins — fewer is faster and safer.

3. Content Updates

- Review recent blog posts and product pages.
- Fix outdated information, prices, or expired offers.
- Add new internal links to recent posts.
- Check images and formatting for mobile readability.

4. Security Scan

- Run a malware and vulnerability scan using **Wordfence**, **Sucuri**, or your hosting dashboard.
- Check for failed login attempts or unusual user activity.

5. Broken Links

- Use the **Broken Link Checker** plugin or an online service to find and fix any broken internal or external links.
- Update or remove links to discontinued products or expired pages.

6. Performance Check

- Run a quick test on **GTmetrix** or **Google PageSpeed Insights**.
- Compare results to your last test — if speed drops, review your caching and image optimization settings.

Quarterly Tasks

Every three months, it's time to take a step back and evaluate the bigger picture — how well your site is performing overall.

1. SEO Audit

- Recheck your target keywords using **Google Search Console** or **Ahrefs Free Tools**.
- Identify any pages that dropped in ranking.

- Update your meta titles and descriptions for clarity and relevance.
- Check for duplicate or missing meta tags.

Pro Tip:
Use your blog analytics to identify topics that get traffic but have room for better conversion — then expand or refresh those pages.

2. Analytics Review

- Open **Google Analytics** and compare the last three months to the previous quarter.
- Look at:
    - Top-performing pages
    - Bounce rates
    - Conversion rates
    - Sources of traffic (Google, social, direct, etc.)
- Focus your next quarter's marketing or content plan on what's working best.

3. Design and Usability Review

- Visit your website on desktop, tablet, and phone.
- Make sure everything displays correctly.
- Check for broken images, buttons, or layout shifts after theme or plugin updates.
- Review your contact and order forms — ensure they're still functioning.

4. Marketing Integration

- Review your email opt-ins and lead magnets.
- Test automation workflows — make sure subscribers receive the correct emails.
- Check social media integrations and sharing buttons for functionality.

Annual Tasks

Once a year, give your entire web ecosystem a deep cleaning. Think of this as your site's "annual checkup."

1. Domain and Hosting Renewal

- Confirm your domain registration and hosting plan are renewed.
- Check billing details and expiration dates — losing a domain by accident can be disastrous.
- Evaluate if it's time to upgrade to a faster or more reliable host.

2. Legal Policies and Compliance

- Review and update your **Privacy Policy**, **Terms of Service**, and **Cookie Notice**.
- Ensure you're compliant with current regulations (GDPR, CCPA, or local data laws).
- If you use email marketing, verify that your sign-up forms include proper consent language.

3. Brand Refresh

- Review your homepage and About page. Do they still reflect your brand, mission, and current services?
- Update outdated photos or graphics.
- Revisit your color palette or typography if they feel dated.

4. Full SEO Review

- Re-run your entire site through **Google Search Console** and **Bing Webmaster Tools**.
- Identify any indexing errors or warnings.
- Audit your sitemap and resubmit it if necessary.
- Review structured data (schema markup) for accuracy.

5. Backup System Test

- Restore one backup to a test environment to confirm it's working properly.

- Update your backup schedule or switch plugins if you've outgrown your current system.

Simple Exercise: Your Website Maintenance Log

Create a simple spreadsheet with three columns:
Date | Task | Notes/Next Step

Each time you perform maintenance, log what you did. Over time, this becomes your website's service history — invaluable if you ever need to troubleshoot or hire a developer.

Final Thoughts

Websites age just like anything else. The difference between a forgotten site and a thriving one is regular attention. These small, consistent check-ins will prevent downtime, protect your investment, and keep your site performing at its best for years to come.

Maintenance may not be glamorous — but it's what separates amateurs from professionals. The more care you give your site, the longer it will keep working for you.

Chapter 24 – Expanding Beyond the Basics

Once your website is running smoothly, backed up, and performing well, it's natural to start thinking:

"What's next?"

Expansion doesn't have to mean starting over — it means building on the foundation you've already created. Whether it's adding a membership area, launching a course, going multilingual, or integrating automation tools, the key is scaling **without breaking your design or SEO**.

This chapter will show you how to expand your website strategically — adding power and profit while keeping everything fast, stable, and user-friendly.

Multilingual Sites

If your audience spans different countries or languages, creating a multilingual site can dramatically increase your reach and trust.

But translating your website isn't as simple as using Google Translate — it requires careful planning for SEO, content consistency, and layout.

Recommended Tools

- **WPML (WordPress Multilingual Plugin)** – The industry standard. Reliable but can be heavy on performance.
- **TranslatePress** – Easier setup; you can translate visually from the front end.
- **Polylang** – Lightweight and free option for smaller sites.

Each lets you create language-specific versions of your pages, posts, and menus — keeping SEO metadata consistent across versions.

Best Practices

- Use **subdirectories** (e.g., yourdomain.com/es/) instead of separate domains for simpler management.
- Translate meta titles, descriptions, and image alt tags — not just text.
- Avoid machine translation for key pages; hire a native translator for accuracy and tone.
- Test your design layout in each language, since longer words or different alphabets may shift spacing.

Pro Tip:

Google indexes each language separately. A well-optimized bilingual or trilingual site can outperform single-language competitors in multiple regions.

Membership or Course Platforms

Turning your website into a membership or e-learning platform is one of the most profitable expansions you can make.
It transforms your site from a marketing tool into a **revenue engine** that generates recurring income.

Popular Membership and Course Plugins

- **MemberPress** – Full-featured membership system for gated content, recurring payments, and access control.
- **LearnDash** – Professional-grade learning management system (LMS) for courses, quizzes, and certificates.
- **LifterLMS** – Excellent all-in-one course builder with integrations for WooCommerce and payment gateways.
- **Paid Memberships Pro** – Lightweight solution for simple paid access models.

What to Offer

- Exclusive tutorials, templates, or downloads.
- Online classes or webinars.
- Premium resources for members.
- Coaching or consultation booking areas.

Scaling Tips

- Use a fast host or VPS (shared servers can slow down with logged-in users).
- Compress all media (videos, PDFs, course files).
- Keep checkout simple — Stripe or PayPal are easiest to integrate.
- Consider using a **subdomain** for course content (learn.yourdomain.com) to reduce load on your main site.

Pro Tip:
Before launching, create a small beta group. Their feedback on usability and navigation can save you major headaches later.

API Integrations and Automation Tools

If your website feels like it's running you — instead of the other way around — it's time to introduce automation.

APIs (Application Programming Interfaces) allow different software platforms to "talk" to each other. You don't need to code; tools like **Zapier**, **Make (formerly Integromat)**, and **Pabbly Connect** handle this visually.

Common Automations

- **Lead Management:**
  Send contact form submissions directly to Google Sheets or your CRM (like HubSpot).

- **Email Sequences:**
  Automatically add new customers to Mailchimp or ConvertKit lists.

- **Social Media Posts:**
  Post your new blog article automatically to Facebook, LinkedIn, or Twitter/X.

- **E-commerce Alerts:**
  Send Slack notifications or SMS messages for new WooCommerce orders.

Best Tools for Beginners

- **Zapier** – User-friendly, ideal for connecting 2–3 apps quickly.

- **Make.com (Integromat)** – More powerful for advanced workflows with conditional logic.

- **IFTTT** – Simplest of all, great for one-step automations (like posting Instagram photos to your WordPress blog).

Pro Tip:

Start small — one automation that saves 10 minutes per day is worth it. Build from there once you see the value.

When to Hire a Developer or Agency

There comes a point where "DIY" reaches its limit.
If you're planning complex integrations, high-traffic membership systems, or custom-coded apps, it's time to call in a professional.

When to Bring in Help

- You're adding features beyond plugin capability (custom dashboards, APIs, or data syncing).
- You need speed optimization or server scaling beyond standard hosting.
- Your site has grown large enough that downtime would seriously impact business.
- You need UX design, branding, or automation expertise to expand professionally.

Finding the Right Partner

- Look for developers with **WordPress or WooCommerce certification** and a proven portfolio.
- Ask for examples of sites similar to yours.
- Clarify communication expectations (weekly reports, testing environments, and post-launch support).
- Always request a **staging site** during development — never let someone build directly on your live site.

Pro Tip:

Treat your developer as a long-term partner, not just a contractor. The better they understand your business, the more effectively they can help it grow.

Simple Exercise: Expansion Planning Worksheet

1. Write down three new features you'd like to add this year.

2. Next to each, note the benefit (e.g., "Membership – recurring income," "Translation – reach new markets").

3. Estimate the complexity: *Simple plugin*, *Advanced plugin*, or *Needs developer*.

4. Rank them by ROI — which one will bring the biggest benefit fastest?

5. Create an action plan for your top choice and schedule it into your next quarter's goals.

Final Thoughts

Expanding your website doesn't mean rebuilding it — it means evolving it. Every new feature should serve a purpose: save time, make money, or improve the user experience.

Add only what enhances your brand and audience relationship. Build gradually, test constantly, and scale smart.

A great website doesn't grow by accident — it grows by design. Plan your next step, and let your website evolve alongside your business.

PART VII – LONG-TERM STRATEGY

Chapter 25 – Building an Online Brand

Websites come and go, but brands endure. A true online brand isn't just a logo or color palette — it's a reputation, a voice, and a promise that customers can recognize anywhere they see you.

Your brand is what remains in someone's mind long after they've left your website. It's the trust you build, the consistency you show, and the story you tell.

Consistency Across Web, Email, and Social

The first rule of branding is **consistency**.
Every time a customer interacts with your business — through your website, an email, or a social post — it should feel unmistakably like *you.*

Use the same tone, logo, and message everywhere:

- **Website:** Clean, reliable, professional design that matches your industry.

- **Email:** Use your logo, colors, and personal tone. Always send from your branded email (never a generic Gmail).

- **Social Media:** Match your profile photos, taglines, and banner images to your site design.

When customers can instantly recognize your brand from a color, style, or even the way you write — you've achieved branding mastery.

A Personal Note

I can honestly say I've never lost a customer.
Why? Because I brand everything I do with my **real name** — and I treat every project as a relationship, not a transaction.

HOW TO WEBSITE DESIGN

Once a customer starts working with me, they become more than a client — they become my friend.

That trust doesn't happen overnight; it's built through consistent effort and integrity across everything I do:

- **Glenn Website Design**
  https://glennwebsitedesign.com
- **Glenn Furniture**
  https://glenn-furniture.com
- **Glenn Madden**
  https://glennmadden.com

Each one looks different, but they all reflect the same voice, craftsmanship, and honesty that define my work.

That's the power of personal branding.

Storytelling and Customer Trust

People don't just buy products — they buy stories. Your story explains **why** you do what you do and what values drive your business.

A strong story turns ordinary products into something memorable.

Elements of an Effective Brand Story

1. **Origin** – Where did your idea begin? What problem did you want to solve?
2. **Mission** – What do you stand for beyond making money?
3. **Transformation** – How have your customers' lives improved because of what you offer?
4. **Authenticity** – Speak in your real voice. People sense when something feels corporate or scripted.

Example:
If you build handcrafted furniture, don't just say "high quality wood." Tell the story of the first desk you built — how you sanded it by hand, what inspired the design, and how that process shapes every piece you make today.

Stories like that build emotional connection — and emotion drives buying decisions far more than logic.

Testimonials: Real Stories from Real People

Testimonials are one of the most powerful storytelling tools you can use.
They're social proof that you deliver what you promise.

Include at least three types:

- **Text reviews** with names and photos.
- **Video testimonials** for authenticity and tone.
- **Case studies** showing before-and-after results or client growth.

Ask happy customers to share specific outcomes, like:

"Our site's traffic doubled in two months after working with Glenn Website Design."

Those details carry far more credibility than "great service."

Pro Tip:
Never fake testimonials. One genuine review is worth more than twenty made-up ones.

How to Position Your Brand for Authority

Once you've built consistency and trust, the next step is **authority** — becoming the go-to name in your field. Authority isn't about bragging; it's about showing your experience and helping others without constantly selling.

Ways to Build Authority

1. **Publish Helpful Content:**
   Write guides, tutorials, and case studies. Teach your audience what you know.

2. **Show Your Work:**
   Use project portfolios, photo galleries, or blog updates to display recent work.

3. **Collaborate and Network:**
   Partner with other reputable brands or industry experts for guest posts or joint projects.

4. **Be Active in Communities:**
   Join forums or Facebook groups related to your field. Offer help freely — your reputation will spread.

5. **Earn Mentions:**
   Submit your site to directories, local listings, or press outlets relevant to your industry.

Personal Branding Tip

If your business carries your name — like mine does — every interaction becomes part of your brand story.
Answer emails quickly, deliver on your promises, and treat clients like friends.
Your name becomes a signature of quality — something people remember and recommend.

Simple Exercise: Your Branding Blueprint

1. Write a one-sentence summary of your brand's mission.
2. Choose three words that describe your personality (e.g., *creative, dependable, approachable*).
3. Make sure your website, emails, and social media reflect those same three words.
4. Write your story — why you started, what you stand for, and who you serve.
5. Ask three happy customers for short testimonials and add them to your homepage.

Within a few weeks, you'll notice a shift — your brand will begin to feel unified, confident, and personal.

Final Thoughts

Your website may be the foundation, but your **brand** is the experience people remember. When every detail — your words, design, communication, and follow-up — reflects who you are, you don't need gimmicks. You just need consistency and integrity.

A logo can be copied, but trust cannot.
Build your brand on honesty, service, and story — and you'll never lose a customer.

Chapter 26 – Measuring ROI and Growth

Once your website is live, optimized, and branded, the next big question is:

"Is it really working?"

Design, SEO, and content are all investments — but unless you measure their results, you're just guessing. That's where **ROI (Return on Investment)** comes in.

This chapter will show you how to define measurable goals, track performance through data, and know when it's time to adjust your strategy for even better growth.

Defining Key Performance Indicators (KPIs)

Your **Key Performance Indicators** are the numbers that tell you whether your website and marketing efforts are delivering results.

These will differ depending on your business type, but every successful website tracks a few common metrics.

Common KPIs for Website Success

- **Traffic Growth:** How many people visit your website each month — and whether that number is increasing.

- **Conversion Rate:** The percentage of visitors who take your desired action (buy, subscribe, or contact).

- **Average Order Value (AOV):** How much a customer spends per transaction.

- **Customer Retention Rate:** How often people come back to buy again or engage with your brand.

- **Cost per Acquisition (CPA):** How much you spend on marketing to gain one new customer.

- **Return on Ad Spend (ROAS):** For those using Google Ads or social campaigns, how much revenue each dollar of advertising brings in.

How to Set KPIs That Matter

1. **Start with your goal.** What's the main outcome you want? (sales, leads, memberships, awareness)
2. **Choose 3–5 KPIs** that directly connect to that outcome.
3. **Set a measurable target.** For example:
   o Increase traffic by 20% in six months.
   o Boost conversion rate from 1.5% to 3%.
   o Add 500 new email subscribers this quarter.
4. **Review regularly.** KPIs are living metrics — adjust them as your business evolves.

Pro Tip:
Don't track *everything*. Measure what matters most to your goals, not what looks impressive on paper.

Using Analytics Dashboards to Track Real Results

You can't manage what you can't measure — and today's analytics tools make it easier than ever to monitor performance.

Google Analytics (GA4)

This should already be connected to your site (see Chapter 17).
Inside GA4, you can monitor:

- **User traffic** (how many, from where, and how long they stay).
- **Conversion paths** (what pages lead to sales or contact forms).
- **Demographics and devices** (who your audience is and how they browse).

Set up a **custom dashboard** showing your most important KPIs — like conversions, sessions, and new vs. returning visitors.

Google Search Console

Use this to measure how you're performing in organic search. Look for:

- Top-ranking pages and keywords.
- Click-through rate (CTR) for each query.
- Errors or pages not being indexed properly.

E-commerce & Email Metrics

If you use **WooCommerce**, you can track revenue, repeat customers, and abandoned carts.
Combine that with **Mailchimp** or **MailerLite** data to see how your email campaigns influence sales.

All-in-One Dashboards

If you'd rather see everything in one place, try:

- **Databox** – Connects to Google Analytics, Search Console, and more.
- **Google Looker Studio (formerly Data Studio)** – Free customizable reports.
- **Zoho Analytics** – Great for multi-channel marketing dashboards.

These platforms visualize your data clearly so you can make quick, informed decisions.

Pro Tip:

Schedule a recurring reminder (monthly or quarterly) to check your dashboards. A five-minute review can reveal trends you might otherwise miss.

When to Pivot Your Content or Business Strategy

Even the best websites need adjustment.
Markets evolve, trends shift, and customer expectations change. What worked six months ago might not work today.

Signs It's Time to Pivot

- Traffic is steady, but conversions are dropping.
- Bounce rates are high on key landing pages.
- Your target audience has shifted (new demographics or interests).
- Competitors are outranking you with newer, more focused content.
- You're spending more time on low-return tasks.

When this happens, it's not failure — it's feedback.

How to Pivot Effectively

1. **Revisit your KPIs.** Make sure they still align with your current goals.
2. **Re-analyze your audience.** Use analytics to identify who's visiting and what they want most.
3. **Review your best content.** Expand what works; retire what doesn't.
4. **Test new approaches.** A/B test your landing pages, CTAs, or pricing to find improvements.
5. **Refocus marketing efforts.** Invest more in the channels (SEO, email, social) that consistently bring results.

Pro Tip:

Don't make major changes all at once. Track one adjustment at a time so you can clearly see what made the difference.

Simple Exercise: Your ROI Tracker

Create a simple spreadsheet with the following columns:

Month | Total Visitors | Conversions | Conversion Rate | Revenue | Marketing Spend | ROI %

- Fill it in monthly using data from Google Analytics and your payment processor.

- Use the formula:

$$ROI = \frac{(Revenue - Marketing\ Spend)}{Marketing\ Spend} \times 100$$

- Aim for steady improvement — even small monthly gains add up over time.

Final Thoughts

Tracking performance isn't about numbers for the sake of numbers. It's about clarity — knowing what's working, what's not, and where to go next.

Your website is a living system. The better you understand its behavior through data, the faster you can adapt and grow.

Design builds attention.
Content builds trust.
But measurement builds momentum — and momentum is what turns a website into a business.

Chapter 27 – Common Mistakes and Lessons Learned

Every web designer, from the newest beginner to the most experienced professional, has made mistakes. The difference between amateurs and professionals isn't perfection — it's how quickly you **learn** from those mistakes and apply the lesson.

After more than 25 years of watching the web evolve — from hand-coded HTML to AI-generated content — I've seen the same patterns repeat. Whether it's overcomplicating a site, neglecting updates, or redesigning without purpose, the result is the same: lost time, lost traffic, and lost trust.

This chapter reveals the most frequent pitfalls, shows real-world examples (including a few from major corporations), and shares the lessons I've learned through experience and observation.

Case Studies of Failed and Successful Sites

Case 1 – The Overbuilt Website

A client once hired me to fix a site that took nearly 30 seconds to load.
It looked beautiful — full of sliders, animations, and videos — but it was collapsing under its own weight. Seventy plugins were doing what five could have handled.

We stripped it down, optimized the code, compressed the images, and removed half the scripts.
The load time dropped to two seconds and conversions tripled.

Lesson: More isn't better. Simple, fast, and functional always beats flashy and slow.

Case 2 – The Neglected Business Site

Another client hadn't logged into WordPress for three years. The SSL certificate expired, the contact form broke, and Google flagged it as "Not Secure."

By the time they called, rankings had vanished and customers stopped trusting the site.

A few updates and a fresh redesign brought it back, but rebuilding credibility took months.

Lesson: A website isn't a "set it and forget it" project — it's a living system that needs regular care.

Case 3 – The Simple Success

One of my smallest projects — a single-page site for a local craftsman — still brings daily leads.

No fancy graphics, no complex structure, just clear photos, pricing, and quick load time.

He updates it faithfully and answers every inquiry personally.

That site outperforms national competitors with 100-page catalogs.

Lesson: Clarity and consistency outperform complexity every time.

Lessons from Big Names: Even Giants Slip

It's easy to think only small businesses make mistakes — but history shows that even major corporations have stumbled publicly online.
The difference is whether they learned and adapted.

Example 1: Healthcare.gov (U.S. Government, 2013)

When the Affordable Care Act's official site launched, millions tried to sign up — and it crashed. Pages froze, logins failed, and users couldn't enroll.

Why it failed:

- No realistic load or stress testing
- Complex code from multiple contractors
- Rushed deadlines that skipped quality assurance

How they fixed it:

A "tech rescue team" was brought in to stabilize the system, rewrite core functions, and phase the rollout instead of doing it all at once. Within months, the platform was stable and functional.

Lesson: Never launch without testing. Roll out in stages, not all at once.

Example 2: Hertz's $32 Million Website Overhaul

Hertz hired Accenture to rebuild its digital experience. After spending tens of millions, the company received unfinished, non-functional systems and sued the agency for breach of contract.

Why it failed:

- Scope creep and unclear deliverables
- No milestone validation
- Lack of accountability between management and developers

How they fixed it:

Hertz terminated the contract, rebuilt key components internally, and simplified its digital roadmap. They shifted to smaller, agile updates instead of one massive rebuild.

Lesson: Big budgets can't fix bad communication. Clear goals and incremental progress are worth more than fancy presentations.

Example 3: Gap's Logo Redesign (2010)

Gap replaced its iconic blue-box logo with a modern version —
and the internet revolted. Within six days, the company
reverted to its old logo after public backlash.

Why it failed:

- Ignored emotional connection customers had to the
  brand
- No focus-group testing or gradual rollout
- Tried to modernize identity without purpose

How they fixed it:
They reinstated the old design, acknowledged the mistake
publicly, and later made only subtle updates that respected the
brand's heritage.

Lesson: Branding changes need testing and communication.
Familiarity and trust often outweigh "freshness."

Example 4: Cracker Barrel's Logo Redesign (2025)

What happened:

Cracker Barrel, an iconic U.S. restaurant and country-store chain, unveiled a new logo in August 2025. The redesign removed the familiar "Uncle Herschel" figure leaning against the barrel, replacing it with a simpler text-based design within a barrel-shaped background.

The reaction was furious. Customers on social media and longtime fans accused Cracker Barrel of abandoning its heritage. The stock dropped more than 10 %.

In response to the backlash, the company quickly issued a statement promising to **bring back the "Old Timer"** figure and reinstate the classic logo.

Moreover, they suspended broader remodeling plans while they reconsider branding and interior design changes.

How they fixed it:

- Reverted the new logo and returned to the old design.
- Committed to retaining the "Uncle Herschel" character in signage, menus, and store décor.
- Paused renovating other restaurant interiors to reassess the direction.

Lesson:

Even when your intentions are modern and your goals are growth, altering core brand elements — particularly ones people attach emotion to — is risky. Transparency, phased changes, and listening to feedback are essential.

Cracker Barrel's reversal illustrates that even large legacy brands must move with humility and respect for customer sentiment.

What to Watch for When Scaling or Redesigning

Growth brings opportunity — and risk. Keep these common traps in mind when expanding:

1. **Losing Your Identity:** Don't abandon your brand's voice or color scheme chasing trends.

2. **Ignoring SEO:** Always redirect old URLs during redesigns. One missed redirect can erase years of ranking.

3. **Underestimating Content Migration:** Plan and test before moving between platforms.

4. **Skipping Testing:** Check forms, carts, and mobile displays before launch.

5. **Scaling Without Infrastructure:** Upgrade hosting before spikes in traffic.

6. **Forgetting Analytics:** Reinstall tracking tools after major updates to keep visibility on performance.

Lessons from 25 Years of Web Evolution

After decades of launches, relaunches, and new technologies, here's what never changes:

- **Trends fade — principles last.** Clean design, clear writing, fast load times, and trust always win.

- **Automation helps — authenticity wins.** AI assists, but people connect to people.

- **Content is king — but context is the kingdom.** Serve the right content at the right time.

- **Relationships outlive algorithms.** Loyal customers will outlast any platform update.

- **Simplicity equals scalability.** The simpler the structure, the easier it is to grow.

- **Keep learning.** The web never stops evolving — and neither should you.

Simple Exercise: Your Website Reflection

1. List three mistakes you've made with your site.
2. Write what caused each one.
3. Record how you fixed or will fix them.
4. Review this list yearly — it will show how much progress you've made.

Final Thoughts

Mistakes are not failures — they're feedback.
Every error teaches something no tutorial ever could.

After 25 years in this business, I've learned that online success isn't about avoiding mistakes — it's about fixing them fast, learning constantly, and staying true to your purpose.

The web changes every day. Integrity doesn't.
Build with honesty, adapt with experience, and your website will keep evolving right alongside you.

Chapter 28 – The Future of Web Design

The web has come a long way from blinking text and table layouts. Today's sites are fast, intelligent, and often built with tools that would have looked like science fiction in the 1990s.

But while technology keeps changing, one truth remains: **people don't want to be treated like machines**.

This chapter looks ahead — at AI design, Web 3.0, and immersive experiences — while reminding you that the future of web design will always depend on the human heart behind it.

AI-Assisted Workflows (Text, Design, Analytics)

Artificial intelligence is transforming nearly every part of web development. Designers now work *with* machines, not against them.

How AI is Reshaping Workflow

- **Content creation:** Tools like ChatGPT and Jasper can generate articles, SEO copy, and marketing messages in minutes.

- **Design assistance:** Platforms such as Wix ADI and Framer AI automatically build page layouts based on prompts or uploaded assets.

- **Analytics and optimization:** AI-powered dashboards identify user patterns and suggest layout or color changes for higher conversions.

- **Automation:** Routine tasks like tagging images, scheduling posts, or A/B testing can now run autonomously.

The opportunity:

AI frees us from repetitive work so we can focus on creativity, storytelling, and strategy.

The risk:

When overused, AI flattens personality. The best sites of the future will combine machine efficiency with unmistakably human perspective.

Web 3.0, AR/VR, and Immersive Experiences

The next wave of web evolution focuses on decentralization, immersion, and interactivity.

Web 3.0

Web 3.0 aims to give users control over their data through blockchain-based systems. Expect to see:

- **Decentralized authentication** instead of password logins
- **Smart contracts** managing memberships or sales automatically
- **NFT-based ownership** for digital assets and creative content

For designers, it means rethinking user experience: trustless transactions, transparency, and security by design.

AR & VR

Augmented and virtual reality blur the line between digital and physical space:

- Furniture retailers now let customers visualize products in their homes through AR viewers.

- Travel agencies offer 360-degree VR previews of destinations.

- Educational and medical sites use immersive environments for training.

The challenge is accessibility — AR/VR experiences require fast networks and strong hardware, so always provide a "flat" version for users on standard devices.

Pro Tip:
Start simple. Add 3-D viewers or interactive product tours before diving into full VR worlds.

Voice Search, Chatbots, and Personalization

We are moving from typing to talking.
Voice search and conversational interfaces are already part of daily life — Siri, Alexa, and Google Assistant all pull from web data.

Voice and Chat Interfaces

- Optimize for **natural language queries**: people say "Where can I buy handmade lamps near me?" instead of typing "handmade lamps Tulsa."

- Include **structured data** so search engines can easily read and serve your content.

- Use **chatbots** for quick responses — but give them a personality aligned with your brand.

Personalization

AI can customize pages to fit each visitor — recommending products, adjusting layout, or tailoring messages based on browsing history.

The key is transparency. Always let users know how their data is used and allow them to control it.

The Human Touch That AI Can't Replace

Technology can answer questions, but only people can understand feelings. Customer service, empathy, and trust still decide who wins online.

A Personal Experience

I've dealt with both extremes.
When I call a company and get trapped in a maze of automated prompts, or worse, outsourced to a call center halfway around the world, I can feel the disconnect immediately. That's **corporate thinking** — efficient on paper, frustrating in practice.

My best support experience was years ago with **iPower**. Their live-chat agents always responded instantly and solved problems without delay. I stayed with them for years because of that personal connection, even though other parts of their service fell behind.

Eventually, their failure to upgrade PHP and address security pushed me to move on — they'd run outdated servers for more than two years. They tried to upsell me with promises that "the upgrade is coming next month," but by then my trust was gone.

I moved to **DreamHost**, and the platform difference was immediate — faster, cleaner, more modern.

But on my first day there, I realized their support wasn't as fast or personable as iPower's used to be. It reminded me that **technology and performance matter**, but so does **relationship and response**.

Lesson learned:
Customers have their limits. A website can automate everything except caring.

Ethical Design and Accessibility

As automation grows, so does responsibility.
Design with empathy:

- Ensure your site meets **accessibility standards (WCAG 2.1)** so everyone can use it.
- Be transparent about AI-generated content and data collection.
- Avoid manipulative "dark-pattern" design that tricks users into clicks.

Ethical design isn't a trend — it's a competitive advantage.
Trust is the new currency of the digital era.

Simple Exercise: Future-Proof Your Site

1. Test how your site reads on **voice search**.
2. Try one **AI tool** for content, layout, or analytics — note what saves time.
3. Add or plan an **immersive element** (360° image, AR model, or product video).
4. Review your **accessibility score** using tools like WAVE or Google Lighthouse.
5. Write one paragraph describing how your business keeps the *human touch* as technology evolves.

Final Thoughts

The future of web design isn't purely technical — it's emotional. AI will help us build faster, smarter, and cheaper, but connection, empathy, and integrity will always set the best designers apart.

Machines can design the structure.
Only humans can design the experience.

The tools will keep changing. The mission won't:

Create spaces online where people feel seen, supported, and inspired — no matter how advanced the code behind it becomes.

Conclusion – The Timeless Code of Design

When I first started building websites in the late 1990s, everything was simple — and complicated — at the same time.

We wrote raw HTML by hand, guessed at browser compatibility, and prayed our images would load before visitors got impatient and left. There were no drag-and-drop builders, no WordPress themes, no AI. Just creativity, persistence, and a burning curiosity about what was possible.

Looking back now, it's amazing how much has changed — and how much hasn't. The languages evolved, the platforms expanded, and the screens got smaller and faster, but the principles stayed the same.

A good website still comes down to the same five things it always has:

1. **Clarity** — People need to know what you do within seconds.
2. **Speed** — Every extra click or second costs trust.
3. **Design** — Beauty still matters, but simplicity converts.
4. **Consistency** — Across pages, platforms, and promises.
5. **Care** — Behind every website is a person serving another person.

These truths outlasted every technological revolution I've seen.

From Code to Connection

I've worked with clients across industries and continents. Some had big budgets; others could barely afford hosting. But in every case, success came down to one thing — **connection**.

A website isn't a collection of pages. It's a conversation. You're speaking to someone who's looking for help, reassurance, or inspiration.

If they feel seen and understood, you've succeeded — whether they buy today or not.

The internet may be full of automation, but real success online still depends on human warmth.

You can't outsource sincerity, and you can't program empathy. That's why I still put my name on everything I build — because people connect to people, not platforms.

What the Next 25 Years Will Bring

We're heading into a world of AI-generated content, voice-controlled browsing, decentralized data, and immersive 3-D experiences.

It's exciting — and overwhelming — all at once.

But here's my prediction:
In 25 years, the designers who thrive won't be the ones who know every new tool. They'll be the ones who remember why they started — to make something useful, beautiful, and meaningful.

Technology changes. Human nature doesn't.
People will always want to feel heard, respected, and valued.

That's why design will always need a human hand — to balance logic with emotion, precision with story, and innovation with understanding.

My Hope for You

If you've made it this far through the book, you're serious about building something that lasts.
My hope is that you now see website design not as a checklist, but as a craft — one that blends technology, psychology, art, and service.

Whether you're building for yourself, your business, or your clients, remember:

- Always test, learn, and improve.
- Keep your systems clean, your code updated, and your backups current.
- Use AI and automation wisely — as partners, not replacements.
- Treat every visitor like a potential friend, not just a conversion.

And above all, never stop creating.

Final Words

After 25 years of this work, I can tell you with certainty — the internet rewards integrity. Every honest effort you make online will find its way back to you in ways you can't predict.

So build with heart.
Design with purpose.

And remember that every click, every visit, and every interaction starts with trust — the one thing no algorithm can manufacture.

The future will always belong to the creators who care.
Keep building. Keep learning. And keep it human.

— Glenn Keith Madden
Glenn Website Design
https://glennwebsitedesign.com

www.ingramcontent.com/pod-product-compliance
Lightning Source LLC
Chambersburg PA
CBHW031239050326
40690CB00007B/870